FINANCIAL CRISIS AND REGULATORY REFORMS

THE BASEL STORY TO TAXPAYERS

SRICHANDER RAMASWAMY

Disclaimer: The opinions expressed in this book are those of the author and do not represent the views of the Bank for International Settlements or other former employers of the author in the official sector.

Cover photo by Michael Chui

First paperback edition 2017

ISBN 978-3-9524785-0-9 (Paperback)
ISBN 978-3-9524785-1-6 (eBook)

Distributed by IngramSpark

This book is dedicated to my mother for teaching me the virtues of humility and honesty; for lending me her ears whenever I needed them; for providing me encouragement and support in times when all odds seemed to be stacked against me; and for guiding me to take the path in life where I can be of help rather than a burden to society.

CONTENTS

PREFACE

Finance and economics were not my subjects of study. Financial markets did not interest me when I was a graduate student and I had neither the time nor the talent for speculation. But destiny dragged me into this field and I spent a good 20 years of my career working with traders, risk managers, central bankers and economists. Looking back I have not regretted this at least for one reason. That is for the insights I gained working on policy and regulatory responses with central bankers following the financial crisis which has enriched my knowledge.

Even today I get occasional questions about the financial crisis from my friends who happened to have just read another book on this topic. During these conversations my friends might mention several names of Wall Street bankers they had learned from their new book. I was always lost during these conversations as I have a poor memory for names, but what intrigued me most was that often I simply could not understand what financial crisis they were talking about.

Sometime in the fall of 2016 I decided to write book about what I understood of the financial crisis and what the driving factors were as a means to avoid these unpleasant conversations. Because I could now refer them to my book and it would contain no names that I need to remember. As a departure from existing books on financial crisis, I decided to wear my engineers' hat and pretended to be investigating the causes of a plane crash. For this mission, it is not important to know the names of the passengers or the flight crew members. What the investigation would normally do is to figure out from the black box the sequence of events that led to the crash and also gather the warning signals that flashed but were ignored or ascertain if they flashed too late to avoid the disaster.

Having decided the strategy of how I want to present the events surrounding the financial crisis, I was confronted with the question of who the target audience for the book will be. Perhaps it will be my fellow engineers and scientists? I know they do not like to read prose and that they will be quickly bored if there are too few equations illustrating my ideas. Perhaps the economists I bumped into during my accidental career? Well, they never seemed to agree to anything I said or others said.

I then felt that my target audience should be taxpayers because it was their money that was used to rescue failing banks and to restore order in the financial markets. As I was some chapters through the book, I quickly realised how complex the story gets if I have to do some justice to the crash investigation. Much of it is related to the financial terminology and arcane regulatory rules that banking supervisors check for compliance. For a deeper understanding of the causes of the financial crisis, knowledge of many topics is needed including financial mathematics, risk management, regulatory rules, accounting standards and behavioural economics. That certainly is expecting too much from every taxpayer. Still, by providing simple examples in a number of places, I hope the book will appeal to a broad audience and help them understand what happened, why it happened and what has been done to prevent this happening.

The book starts as a memoir recollecting the events how I ended up in the banking industry rather than realising my dreams of building aircrafts and missiles after completing my doctoral thesis in aerospace engineering. Chapters 2 and 3 provide background information about financial markets and the Bank for International Settlements which hosts meetings for central bankers to coordinate regulatory policies. Chapter 4 is a primer on Basel II standards that some have blamed for the crisis. These chapters are essential reads for those with limited knowledge of financial markets.

The chapters 5 to 11 describe the events leading to the crisis and how regulatory rules and the financial architecture have been redesigned to build a safer financial system with a core element being that taxpayer money will not be available if banks get into trouble again. In the final chapter I provide my personal views on the challenges that lie ahead and some suggestions on how to address them.

Srichander Ramaswamy
Basel, March 2017

What we have learned is a mere handful.

What we have not learned is of the size of this world.

Auvaiyar, 4th Century Tamil poet from India

CHAPTER ONE

BERLIN DAYS

It was still very cold when I arrived in Berlin in March 1993 from Chennai. It was not my first encounter with cold weather. I was used to sub-zero temperatures in winter while living in the mid-West in the United States when I was a grad student. But it takes a few days to get used to the cold weather when you arrive from a place with tropical climate.

Ignoring my discomfort I told my wife, "I am so happy to be back in Berlin" as I unpacked my bags. I had spent a few months in Berlin around Christmas time in 1991, so it was like returning to a city I knew well. There were so many places I did not manage to visit or explore during my first trip. With spring approaching, I knew the next few months will be packed with explorations and expeditions to places of historical interest.

"I have applied for a bigger apartment" my wife reassured me as I glanced around looking for a place to keep my suitcases. The 20 square meters apartment was small for two of us, but the prospect of moving soon to a 35 square meters apartment sounded very promising. Life cannot treat us better I thought.

After briefly sharing the joy of being reunited after six months, we had to make plans as regards how I will go about looking for a job in Berlin. Improving my knowledge of German was a pre-requisite if I was to realise that dream. But I knew that it will take me considerable time given my poor skills in learning a foreign language.

To deflect my attention from this unpleasant reality, I decided to switch topics. "When are we visiting the war museums in East Berlin?" I enquired as we settled down to chat.

Germans were always uncomfortable talking about the war period, and that was not new to me. I had no particular emotional attachment to developments during that period growing up in India. But I liked history, and I wanted to learn more about a watershed moment in Europe and to visit the remains of places that capture those moments. There was no better place than Berlin where I could begin my interrogation and enquiries to gain an alternative perspective on the tragedies of war than what is portrayed in the Hollywood films.

"Let us postpone that trip to the summer as there are other interesting places to visit in the neighbourhood" my wife said. The matter was settled as I did not want to disagree with her on the first day.

The following days I unpacked all my graduation certificates and prepared to get copies of them to send with my cover letter and resume to prospective employers. The German companies insisted on having your picture attached to the resume and to enclose all certificates for verification. As the German companies and universities did not recognise an American degree, I was instructed to get it officially certified by a German government institution as being equivalent to a German degree certificate. After a few weeks of hard work, I managed to get my act in order to be able to tackle the cumbersome German bureaucracy.

Over the following months, my optimism of getting a job in Germany started waning. The Germans back then were used to hiring foreigners mostly in the services sector as guest workers. The companies I applied to could not quite comprehend what tasks they could give to me if I was confined to desk work. The Germans were trained to do that sort of work and with the reunification of Germany there were plenty of them who were interested in these jobs.

Months passed by during which I was scanning every newspaper for potential jobs that I could apply to. In the summer I visited my in-laws living near Frankfurt. By that time I had already perfected my German through intense learning, an outcome that even surprised me. My mother-in-law took note of that and appreciated my talent for languages even though I was convinced I had none. "Many foreigners do not manage to speak a few proper sentences in German even after living several decades here," she remarked.

The conversation quickly shifted to the efforts I was taking to find a job. "It has been a difficult process," I told her trying to be diplomatic.

"It does not surprise me," she replied. "There are so many intelligent Germans who are unemployed after the wall came down. No one will prefer to hire an Indian when they can employ a German, and it will be very difficult for you to find a job here."

That captured the mood of the average German I encountered in my everyday life. People I met on the streets were polite and friendly, especially when you can speak proper German sentences. They all said they liked Indian food, but I told them I cannot cook. That disappointed some. But these conversations helped me gauge the mood of Germans towards foreigners as any mention of my intent to find a job in Germany was met with scepticism.

The truth was that I had a job but was not being paid. A month after arriving in Berlin, I decided to meet with the professor for control systems engineering at the Technical University. That was the subject I had studied in my master's program and was also the topic of my doctoral thesis in the department of Aerospace Engineering. My wife gave me a stern warning that I should first try to fix an appointment with his secretary and not to drop in his office without warning. As a student at the Free University, she knew how to respect the hierarchy of German professors. Typical advance notice time required was at least one week to get an appointment.

Waiting for one week for an appointment seemed eternal to me. I did not make an appointment if I wanted to meet briefly with my thesis adviser in the United States. And before coming to Berlin, I was teaching at an Indian University. So I did not feel inferior to a professor even if I did not hold the title at that point in time. While I could see why an undergraduate student may need an appointment, I was convinced this constraint should not apply to me. So I went straight up to the friendly secretary and asked if I could meet for five minutes with the professor.

"He should have time now," she said confidently and called to check. "Please go in, Professor Hartmann has time for you," she said hanging up the phone.

I walked in to Professor Hartmann's office and we greeted each other. Both of us subsequently struggled for words – he could barely speak English and I could barely speak German. But over the next ten minutes I managed to explain to the professor the research topics I have worked on, the journal articles I have published, and the professors I have worked with. As I quickly glanced at his book shelf, he had some books that were written by the Indian professors I had worked with whose names I had mentioned.

It is hard to judge what went in his mind during that brief encounter. All I remember is that he was apologetic and said he has no funds to support me because getting research grants had become extremely difficult after the reunification. But he could make me an offer. There was a vacant room in the department, and he said he would be very pleased to give me the keys to the room. I could also use the departmental library facilities and assume the title of guest scientist.

I thanked him for his offer and said that in return I can do some research seminars for masters and doctoral students. As we walked out of his office, he instructed his secretary to hand over the keys to the vacant room and to the departmental library. When I received the keys, it was like manna falling from heaven. It was an act of extraordinary friendship and trust from a German professor that would never escape my memory.

There was no mobile telephone those days to call my wife and share my joy. When I told her my story in the evening and the fact that I have an office at the Technical University, she did not want to believe me. "Why did you not follow my instructions to fix an appointment first?" she argued. My non-German way of doing things did not please her. But I decided to ignore her displeasure. I was not used to taking instructions from anyone, and I had no plans to change that habit.

Over the course of the next nine months I sent dozens of applications to prospective employers. Within two weeks every one of them was returned, often with the remark that I am over-qualified for the job. Over-qualified? That word did not exist in my vocabulary. I knew that you could be either qualified or not qualified for a job. But the German language seemed to be richer.

In the meanwhile I decided to spend more time working on interesting research projects I had in mind. Back in India, I had worked on a project to design the automatic controller for a fighter aircraft that was being developed. I had also done research work for the US Airforce Office of Scientific Research on detecting failures in aircrafts, and to adjust control laws to ensure safe return of aircrafts after battle damage to the airbase. Designing fault tolerant control laws and deriving the conditions for stability of jump vector stochastic non-linear differential equations was the topic of my doctoral thesis.

The research projects kept me going. I managed to send two papers to reputed engineering journals on solving an aircraft controller design problem by employing a modified simulated annealing optimisation algorithm I developed. Both papers were accepted after a first review. I was delighted and decided to present these ideas in a research seminar at the Technical University. Unfortunately, only two of my friends turned up for the seminar on the proposed date. Germans after all were practical minded people. They had exited the business of designing aircrafts and missiles 70 years back. It was a stark reminder that the hurdles to cross were becoming insurmountable.

I was not someone who will give up on hopes easily. As an enthusiastic cricketer having played for my school and university teams that included members who subsequently represented the Indian team, I knew no game is lost until the last ball is bowled. Reassurances came from my mother. She had consulted a well-known astrologer in Chennai who had asserted that I will have a job in August 1994. There was less than five months to go. My brother was less confident of relying on astrology. "Have you tried applying to banks?" he enquired.

"What on earth will I do in a bank?" I retorted. I knew something about banks. On many occasions while I was in school my father had sent me to withdraw money from a bank by handing over a cheque. I had also learned to hand over the savings book to the clerk to make a hand written entry of the interest money credited. Someone told me that banks could give loans to businesses. Banks in India, however, were not authorised to give loans for buying houses those days. I simply could not understand how my engineering education and mathematical prowess could be useful for such a mundane business.

"I read in the newspapers that Wall Street banks are hiring physicists and engineers," my brother continued from the other side of the Atlantic. I could only vaguely remember someone uttering the word Wall Street in 1987 after the stock market crash when I was in the United States. I did not bother to ask what it meant or where it was as my mind was fixated on the few hundred dollars in my bank account that I needed to get through the month.

"Are these banks like the State Bank of India?" I asked him. That was the only large bank I could relate to where my father kept his accounts. My question did not surprise my brother as he knew my imagination did not go far beyond mathematics and cricket.

"Let me explain," he said. "These banks trade in stocks and bonds and sell some financial products that are dependent on the prices of those stocks and bonds. I gathered that to price these financial products you need to have good skills in stochastic calculus and computer programming." The technical terms he used were familiar to me, and I knew both very well. With few other options available, I felt it might be time to refocus my mind from building fighter planes to helping banks price financial products. And over time I can figure out what those financial products are. For once I did not dismiss my brother's suggestion of looking for job advertisements from banks in newspapers.

A few weeks passed and I now had a new mission. I had to look additionally for the key word "banks" in job advertisements. Buying newspapers was expensive, so I usually went to a library where I could get hold of one. My favourite library was in East Berlin which kept multiple copies of newspapers and you could get hold of one in less than an hour's wait. On that day, sometime in late March, I managed to grab my favourite newspaper, the Frankfurter Allgemeine Zeitung, as I walked in.

I always took my time going over the advertisements. No one in Berlin seemed to be in a hurry either. While slowly looking for the right buzz words as I navigated the difficult German language text, something very strange caught my eye. There was an advertisement in English in the German newspaper. "Have the Germans gone crazy?" was the first thing that occurred to me. I decided to take a closer look as I could read it with ease. It did not have the buzz word "bank" in it that I was looking for. But it said "Schweizerische Kreditanstalt is looking for engineers and scientists to price FX options and other derivatives." I simply could not tell what business this institution was doing. Moreover, the institution was in Zurich.

I was puzzled and read the advertisement twice. I had no idea what FX and derivatives meant. Language was not an issue but terminology was. All I knew is that I could comfortably wear the hat of an engineer or a scientist. I decided to take a copy of the advertisement and find out later what the institution's business is.

During the subway ride back home, many thoughts came to my mind. Why does a Swiss firm want to advertise for engineers and scientists in Germany? Perhaps the Swiss engineers and scientists are not as intelligent as their German counterparts? I knew the Germans will not object to this view. But I did not want to entertain that idea. If they were serious about recruiting German engineers and scientists, why would they advertise in English? My sixth sense told me that the target audience of that advertisement was non-Germans. Could the astrologer be right? I knew I had homework to do in the next few days.

There was no google search available those days to answer my queries. So I called my brother to find out if he knows anything about this institution in Zurich. He was quick to figure out after I read the advertisement to him that it must be one of the two large Swiss banks headquartered in Zurich. There was no time to be wasted, and I got down to writing my covering letter and sending my standard application pack. Three weeks passed by and I almost forgot about this job I applied for. I was back to my routine of working on my research and going to the library during the weekends to scan newspapers for advertisements.

One evening as I was preparing to fix my dinner the phone rang in my apartment. I knew it must be a call for my wife as no one usually called me. And my brother would never call at this time. I was reluctant to pick it up as my wife was away, but after four rings I decided to answer the phone. The lady on the phone called out my name and enquired if that person was me. She said she was calling from Zurich following up on the application I sent.

After the standard exchange of formalities, she wanted to ask some technical questions about my background. After 15 minutes the matter was settled. I was told that I will receive an invitation to come to Zurich for an interview. She also assured me that the bank will send me an invitation letter to apply for a visa and that the flight tickets will be mailed to me.

Everything worked out with Swiss precision as I arrived at their head office in Zurich. The weather was great as it was already end-April. But I was quite nervous as I did not know what they were expecting from me. The knowledge I had about banks at that time was how to withdraw and deposit money into my account. While being taken inside the building, I realised that this bank was very different from the ones I had seen in India.

Walking with me to the division's office, the lady, who had earlier spoken to me over the phone, made me feel at ease. She assured me that the interview is not about testing what I do not know, but what I know. When I met her Finnish boss, he welcomed me and said he had worked with Indians and was always impressed by their intelligence and hard-working nature. That reassured me and my confidence returned.

During the rest of the day there were several rounds of interviews. The purpose was to test my technical and social skills, ability to work in a team, adaptability, and most importantly, willingness to work in a completely different field. I managed to score well on all of them. But the final interview round with the head of the unit turned out to be the toughest. Not because he asked me a difficult technical question. I could have answered that. On the contrary, he asked me a simple question: "What do you know about FX derivatives?"

I thought that someone has to call out that the emperor has no clothes. He was best placed to do that. I decided to be frank but make the point that I am a fast learner. "I do not know what they are," I told him. "But I am a fast learner, and if you give me a month's time, I will learn the terminology."

He seemed prepared for that answer based on the feedback he got from those who had interviewed me. "Never mind," he said. "I have discovered that it is easier to teach someone with strong math skills finance rather than the other way round." He then pulled out a book from his shelf and handed it to me and asked, "How long will it take you to read and understand the material in the book?"

I flipped the pages in the book to see what it contained. It was more than 450 pages in length and contained plenty of equations and formulas. But I quickly recognised the similarity of those equations with the engineering literature I was familiar with. There were sections on use of numerical methods to find solutions, again all too familiar as I had done courses in those and had even given lectures to masters' students in applying these methods for engineering problems. After a few minutes I returned the book to him and said that it will take me two weeks to read and understand the material covered in the book.

I came to know later that the book, "Options, futures and other derivatives" by John Hull was considered to be a difficult read, and was taught over two semesters to masters' students in mathematical finance. There was brief silence after I handed over the book. Then the boss smiled, stood up and shook my hands. After a brief exchange of formalities, I started my journey to the airport feeling relaxed that the agony is over.

Still, many thoughts crossed my mind as I took my seat in the plane and looked out at the Alps from the window. Having done many courses in probability theory, I wondered what I would tell my wife if she asks me how I assess my chances of getting the job. Perhaps 5 percent, 10 percent or even 50 percent? That will depend, I thought, on how many smart German engineers and scientists had applied for this position. But why would a Finn, Filipino, Britt, American and Canadian ever come up with the idea that a German is smarter than an Indian?

I felt very relieved with my self-assessment of how my interviewers' minds might work. As I pondered over my destiny, I was interrupted by a gentle voice and a seductive smile from a pretty young German stewardess. "Would you like to have a glass of wine?"

After I returned to Berlin, it was business as usual. As I counted my pennies with the month-end approaching, my wife reminded me to be thrifty. "We will soon run out of our savings," she said. The government stipend she was receiving was barely enough to meet both our needs.

To escape the realities of life, I set out to complete another research paper that I was working on to present at an international conference in Copenhagen to demonstrate how wind shear and wind gust can affect algorithms that try to detect failures in aircraft sensors. But on the job front, I was slowly getting tired of searching for advertisements in newspapers.

It was already early June, and in a few weeks' time I was supposed to travel to Copenhagen to present my paper in the conference. I was hoping to meet some professors there and explore if they had research grants to support me at their institute. But that day in early June we were having a party and I only had time to pick up my mail from the post box. There was big envelope from Zurich, but I was convinced that my application material was being returned, a practice followed in the German-speaking world. I decided not to open the envelope and spoil my mood during the party.

When I finally got the time to open the envelope, I was overwhelmed with joy to see the job offer from the Swiss bank. There was still one more hurdle to cross. The bank had to apply for a work permit once I returned the signed contract, and then I had to wait patiently with the hope that the state will grant the permit.

But within a week, the young lady from Zurich called again. She thanked me for accepting the offer and enquired if she could mail to me the book I was shown as it would help me to be better prepared when I arrive in Zurich. The book promptly arrived in a few days' time, and in the following two weeks I managed to get a good grasp of every equation contained in the book. And in another week I memorised all the buzz words and financial market jargon contained in it. I knew this is needed to help the transition from designing aircrafts to pricing financial products.

The process to get my work permit took another month. Finally, I had my work visa by end-July. I started my job in Zurich with the title Financial Engineer in the second week of August. My mother went to the astrologer she had consulted and thanked him for his prediction.

CHAPTER TWO

ZURICH EXPERIENCE

The first thing that struck me most as I relocated to Zurich is how courteous and friendly people were in the trams. It seemed like being in a different planet. Everything was more expensive, but it did not bother me now. My first task was to find an apartment. I was very lucky. A few days after my arrival, I found an apartment that was within my budget. The lady living there wanted to rent it for six months in a fully furnished condition. We did the deal and I was pleased that I did not have to worry about buying furniture for some time. But she preferred to inform her landlord before handing the keys. It was just a matter of procedural courtesy she told me.

The next day when she called to inform me, she was extremely apologetic. Her landlord had told her categorically that as a matter of principle he does not rent his apartment to Indians. One of his friends apparently had a bad experience with an Indian family as they tend to cook often and dirty the kitchen. Despite telling him that my wife is not Indian, and being alone I may not be cooking much, his position was uncompromisable. That did not sound like the end of the world to me. The reference to a Swiss bank as my employer was highly valued in the rental market. In a few weeks' time I managed to strike a deal with another landlord.

At work, I had a few days to get familiarised with the computer systems used in the bank. Engineers are trained to adapt quickly to new technology. My American colleague, also an engineer, was extremely helpful in making the transition smooth.

My first assignment came a few days after I joined. I was told that the unit needed a sophisticated estimation algorithm to build smooth yield curves. In lay mans' terms, a yield curve represents the interest rates that one would earn for fixed-term deposits of different maturities. For bond markets, the yield curve representing the term structure of interest rates is like the foundation for a building. One can think of each floor built on top of this foundation to represent a certain type of financial product. As you keep moving up the floors, the complexity of the product increases.

For many, writing software to generate a yield curve may sound trivial. For example, one can simply interpolate to join the points that represent the interest rate for maturities extending from one month onwards in steps of three or six months. But the interdependencies between interest rates of different maturities embedded in prices of traded instruments, such as bonds, require special estimation methods. And more so if the resulting curve is to display some smoothness conditions. But that was a task I was able to complete in a few weeks' time.

More tasks were now being assigned to me after my first success. It was time to turn my attention to pricing options on bonds. But what is the underlying theory that establishes a link between pricing financial instruments and engineering? How did I manage to read a text book in mathematical finance in a few weeks' time? Let me provide some answers to these questions.

We all know that if we deposit $100 in a bank paying 4 percent annualised interest rate, we will have $104 in our account in one year time. But if we had bought $100 worth of Apple or Orange shares and kept it in the securities account, the value at the end of one year could be a range of numbers around $104. How wide can that range be?

Financial economists try to estimate this by using tools developed in probability theory. The famous example used in the class room to explain the range of possible outcomes around $104 is to think of a drunkards' walk. Let us assume that the man leaves the pub after drinking two litres of beer and heads home. At which house door he will knock in the neighbourhood of his home will depend on the level of alcohol in his blood. The more he is drunk, the more likely it is that the house he knocks at will lie further away from his own house. Of course, each night he might end up knocking on a different house door, including sometimes the one he lives in.

Over the course of a year, if one would keep track of every house he tried to enter after returning from the pub, and then measure the average distance of those houses from his house, one would arrive at a measure called the standard deviation. Keeping aside some underlying assumptions, the standard deviation captures the maximum distance on either side of his house within which the drunken man will end up two-thirds of the time. Financial economists are used to calling this statistical outcome "volatility" instead of standard deviation.

One could think of the evolution over time of the Apple share price to be displaying the characteristics of a man who drinks two litres of beer every day before embarking on his journey home. The evolution over time of the Orange share price might display the characteristics of a drunkards' walk who consumes three litres of beer every night. In this case, the volatility of the Orange share price will be greater than that of the Apple share price. Observing past daily prices of a financial instrument will allow us to compute the volatility of that particular financial instrument. The underlying driver of the volatility of stocks of different companies, for example, will be among others their relative share of debt versus equity capital in the companies' balance sheet and the earnings prospects in the particular sector. More debt and greater uncertainty in earnings is equivalent to more alcohol consumption.

The drunkards' walk, known as random walk in probability theory, is a fundamental building block for studying the implications of random disturbances on engineering systems. Turbulences or a short burst of cold air front can be regarded as random disturbances affecting an aircrafts' flight path. Radar signals received in ground stations are often corrupted with other signals that need to be filtered out. These disturbances are modelled as a limiting case of the random walk. That is, rather than a six foot tall drunkard reaching home in 500 footsteps, we need to study the 5000 footsteps needed for a small child walking in darkness to reach the same destination. But the fundamental properties of the random walk process itself do not change as the length of these steps is compressed.

The behaviour of many engineering systems, like an aircraft in flight, can be modelled by laws of physics. The gravity that pulls the aircraft towards the ground, the circulation of air around the wings that counters the gravitational force to provide lift, and the thrust from the jet engines that propel the aircraft forward, all allow a dynamical model of the aircrafts' motion to be established. The evolution of the price of a bond until its maturity follows some laws of economics that is different from laws of physics. But seen in isolation, it will be difficult to distinguish an equation that describes the evolution over time of a variable of economic interest from that of variable which describes some characteristics of an engineering system. This is the glue that helps engineers communicate with financial economists.

Once the equation describing the evolution of a financial variable is formulated together with the properties of the uncertainties or disturbances that affect it, one can trace out a possible outcome for that variable over a given time horizon. In practice, one tries to study the paths taken by several drunkards each having consumed the same quantity of alcohol to make inferences. These random walks can be generated using computer-assisted simulation that embeds the underlying equations capturing the evolution of the financial variables.

Pricing any derivative or option on a financial instrument becomes relatively simple when seen from an engineering perspective. For example, one may think of having trenches on the way home from the pub. If the drunkard deviates too much from the intended path that would be taken by a sober person, he would fall into those trenches. Such trenches can be dug on either side of intended path. If the drunkard falls into the one to the left of his path, he gets knocked-out and will never reach his destination. If he deviates too much to the right hand side, he will be knocked-in. There are financial products that are called knock-out and knock-in options.

A knock-out option on a stock would disqualify an investor from further participation in the spoils of the Wall Street party. A knock-in option would give him the right to enter the party through a particular stock or other financial instruments. The pricing of such options would require examining how many drunkards, out of say

1000, fall into the trench on the left when they return home. Knowing the relative frequency with which the drunkards fall into the trench will allow the bank to calculate the option price a speculator has to pay, which will be a function of the pay-off when the event happens. This is really not rocket science mathematics as any undergraduate engineering student will be able to write a computer program to estimate the price of such an option.

A cautionary tale, however, is needed to highlight potential pitfalls. The bar tender may have good statistics on how many litres of beer each of his customers drink. But you may not have asked him if those statistics are correct on St. Patricks' day when people tend to drink more. Or, he could have started working only six months back and had never seen how many additional beers his customers drink on St. Patricks' day. So, the bar tenders' best guess would be what he has observed during his brief tenure. This will underestimate the relative frequency with which the drunkards will fall into trenches on St. Patricks' day. If the pricing of knock-in and knock-out options fail to account for the St Patricks' day event, there can be significant market disruptions.

There is a lot of jargon though that an engineer has to learn to communicate with traders. Do you want to be long or short the trade? This has no implications for pricing but it helps to establish credibility with the traders. An investor who buys a knock-in option would have the right to receive the payoff when the option contract matures, provided the knock-in condition has been met. For this right, the investor has to pay an upfront fee to the bank offering the product, and the investor will be considered to be long this option. Usually, the trader communicates to the financial engineer from the perspective of his exposure to this trade. The trader's exposure when he executes the trade will be a short position in this option, and he will be liable to making a final payment to the investor if the option kicks-in. The notion of being long or short in a trade is extremely important to determine how the trader will offset or hedge the risk of the exposure in his trading book.

But there are plenty of simpler variants to the knock-in and knock-out options. One could buy or sell a European, American, Asian or Bermudan option. Those could either be a call or a put option. And the strike price, the price at which the option payoff will be activated, has to be negotiated in advance. This arcane Wall Street jargon is what puts off many people at first instance. A call option gives the right to buy at a certain price a financial instrument. For example, you may enter into the option of buying one Microsoft share at $105 in one year time if it trades above this level. In this case, the investor is buying a European call option today for which he has to make a down payment based on an estimate of the volatility of the share over the next one year. Financial engineers pricing these options can estimate this volatility using prices of other options being traded in the market.

American options, in contrast to European options, allow the investor to collect the payoff any time over the life of the option contract when the predetermined condition is met. This makes the price of American options more expensive. Buying one year American put option at the strike price of $95 would allow the investor to sell the Microsoft share to the bank at this price any time over the next one year if the shares trade lower than this price. If, for example, the share price is $90, then the investor can claim $5 from the bank by exercising the put option. The upfront option price he paid will reduce the net profit to the investor.

The payoffs on Asian options are dependent on the average price of the share over the period of the option contract, usually computed based on daily closing prices. As the payoff is dependent on the entire path of the random walk made by the share price over the course of the year, they pose some challenges to traders to hedge these exposures. Therefore, traders charge an additional premium to sell such options.

For an observer, this business of selling or buying options will look very similar to that of a casino that offers games like roulette and blackjack. There is no fundamental difference between the mathematics that establish the price a casino will charge to play a game of roulette or blackjack and the price a Wall Street banker will quote to sell an option on a financial instrument. Both require estimates of the probability of various outcomes and their associated payoffs to determine the participation fee. The casino and the Wall Street bank will normally set the price to ensure that it has a home edge to make the business of offering these games or options profitable.

To provide a concrete example, a casino may offer players a payoff in dollars that is equal to the number that shows up when a dice is thrown. With six sides, the expected value of a throw will result in a payoff of $3.5. This is derived by summing the numbers from one to six, which is equal to 21, and then diving by six, which is the number of sides or outcomes. The casino will break even if it charges the players $3.5 to play the game with the agreed payoff. In practice, the casino will have to cover the operational costs and also provide some dividends to their owners. This may result in the casino charging $3.8 to play the game. The speculator may still be enticed to play this game even if the odds are stacked against him as he may see that there is a 50 percent chance of making some profit. The sums involved in the financial derivatives markets are larger but the principle is the same. There will be winners and losers in this game, but we should not make gods out of the winners.

The example and the arguments given above may lead some to conclude that all financial products offered by banks are sold to speculative investors. Quite to the contrary, there are several simple options and other financial contracts that do help investors or businesses offset or hedge their financial risks. A business that has to pay for a shipment in two months' time in a foreign currency might want to fix the exchange rate it wants to pay to remove uncertainties in its financial planning. A commodity exporter may want to eliminate the fluctuations in price of that commodity at shipment times through good financial planning that will necessitate the buying of hedging products.

An engineer working in a factory producing knifes will focus on the usefulness of the products he helps manufacture to the people working in the kitchen. But the product can also turn out to be dangerous if the knife ends up the hands of an angry young man. The engineer's job ends in the factory. He has no mandate to inform the marketing team what types of people these knifes can be sold to. I was conscious of this trade-off working as an engineer on projects that may end up having destructive power and learned to keep math and sentiment separate. I was determined to keep this tradition as I embarked on my journey to be a financial engineer.

Being a financial engineer meant that you are also a banker. That meant I had to wear a suit every day to office, which I hated.

Confined to my office in a business suit, I now had the new task of building a pricing tool for bond options. My boss told me I should not hesitate to contact him if I had questions as I still had much to learn. The reference book he had given me was very helpful. I had already learned that there are fundamental differences between how options on stocks and bonds are priced. Indeed, I now quickly realised why my first task was to build a model to generate the yield curve by using prices of bonds traded in the market.

As I dug deeper driven by my scientific training to understand the intuition that lay behind the use of the yield curves as the building block for pricing bond options, many things became clearer and I started to see things beyond the simple mathematical models. A particular bond may expire in one year, two years or five years. Assuming the contractual agreements on the bond will be met, meaning timely payment of interest accrued and principal, the bond will display the features of a fixed term bank deposit as it approaches maturity. This introduces complexity in pricing options on bonds because every bond will display different volatility characteristics.

Financial economists circumvent this problem by directly modelling changes in the yield curve. And the yield curve itself is simply a representation of future short-term interest rate expectations. The intuition behind this is that central banks control the short term interest rate, and over a business cycle these short term rates are increased or decreased depending on the state of the economy. Many theoretical models of yield curve are built on this one factor, the short-term interest rate, which is assumed to revert over time to its long-term equilibrium value.

The mathematical formulation of how the yield curve shape evolves over time is more complex than the one that describes the price dynamics of stocks. The shape shifting of the yield curve is modelled by examining how the short-term rates controlled by the central bank will change in one month, three months, one year and so forth from now. The model of the short-term rates in combination with the appropriate random walk imposed on it provides the framework to predict the probabilistic outcomes for the short term interest rates over the following months and years. It turns out that the price of bond is some function of these future short-term interest rates. This link helps to forecast the probabilistic distribution of the price of the bond over its remaining term before expiry.

My task of implementing a model for pricing bond options had boiled down to transforming the various short term rates embedded in the yield curve into bond prices, and then ensuring that the software I was writing had no bugs in it. I managed to get this done in reasonable time. Everyone in my team seemed to be pleased with my progress and appreciated my humility. I gathered from my colleagues that humility is a scarce resource in the investment banking world.

Implementation of the option pricing model was only the first step. It was not mission accomplished. That required, I was told, to speak to traders and get price quotes for traded options on bonds in order to calibrate the two parameters used in the pricing model. The acceptance of the model required figuring out if there are any discrepancies between the option prices it estimated and those that were quoted in the market.

This required a trek to the trading floor. I was told that the traders are very busy people and do not like being disturbed. Moreover, I did not have access to the trading floor. My colleague Cecilia offered to give me a helping hand. She knew the traders on the floor well and was glad to take me on a tour and get me introduced to the bond traders.

The recollection of my first visit to the trading floor was like being in a vegetable market in the streets of Chennai. I had to navigate with great dexterity through one such market on my way to college every day. Vendors were screaming to outsmart the one next to them to sell their products and had slogans to claim why their products were so much better. Some offered difficult-to-ignore discounts that attracted big crowds to these vendors. But my mother had warned me not to heed these sales pitches. There was always a hidden trap, such as the use of unbalanced weighing scales or the vendor bringing his arm into play when holding the scales to tilt it in his favour. "The more marketing a vendor does, the less you should trust the products he sells," my mother often reminded me.

But the investment bankers with their expensive suits gave me the confidence that they were a different bunch. And they sounded as confident as the vegetable vendors about the quality as well as the knowledge of the products they were selling to their customers over the phone. I was impressed and remained optimistic that any question I may ask them on bond options will be answered with great clarity.

We stopped by a trader Cecilia knew well and who also worked for the same unit. There was no time for formalities. Every conversation that resulted in the trader taking his eyes off the computer screen meant lost profits for the bank. Well, at least that is how they acted. So, I decided to get down to business right away.

"I want to have prices of bond options to calibrate an interest rate model I have implemented," I told him. "What bonds are you referring to?" he said annoyed. "I trade options on Treasuries, Bunds and Gilts."

"Well, Treasuries would be good enough for now," I replied being pleased that I can select one item from his jargon.

"What options are you interested in, call or put?"

I noticed that the trader was already showing signs of irritation, but he managed to keep his calm. "I would prefer to have both," I told him to avoid saving another trip to the trader.

"I need to know the strike price. Do you want at-the-money, out-of-the-money or in-the-money?"

Things were now getting out of control. I did not know what I needed to calibrate my option pricing model. Noticing my hesitation, the trader decided to offer me a concession.

"Look," he said. "I will give you prices of at-the-money options because they are more liquid. But you have to tell me what option maturity you want to have. Do you prefer one month, three months or some other maturity?"

At this stage I wanted to go back to the vegetable vendor. I had a full grasp of the products he kept in his sack and knew all the tricks he might pull out of his hat as he tried to sell it to me. This was certainly not the case here. "One month option price is want I want," I told the trader, and was not sure if my judgment was right.

"Do you want the prices for on-the-run or off-the-run Treasuries, and should they be two, five or ten year bonds?"

I noticed that by this time there were many traders around him looking at me very amused and wondering what I was up to.

"Let me come back to you with a more specific request," I told him to cut short my misery. "Good decision," he said, and refocused his attention to the computer screen to exploit the next opportunity to earn a million dollars.

As I returned to my desk, I felt like being dropped in the middle of the Sahara desert with no one to pick up your SOS calls. You had to work out your own strategy for survival. Some tips and encouragement came from my colleagues, but they were also not traders. I grasped the book I had read earlier to search for clues, and I now had a personal copy of it. The book contained standard material one would teach in a classroom, but fell well short of the stuff I needed to communicate with busy traders. Nonetheless, after a few days of intense self-inquiry I managed to write down the complete list of specifications I had to give to the trader to get a bunch of bond option prices.

My second trip to the trader ended in a successful mission and I got a list of bond option prices to calibrate and test my model's accuracy. After some trial and error, I managed to fix the software bugs and ensured that the model met the accuracy needed to make a first demonstration of an in-house model with bond option pricing capabilities.

After a few months I became more familiar with my new working environment and less conscious of running around the city in a business suit. But I needed some relief from this unfamiliar business and strange work culture. I therefore made it a point to spend a good part of my Saturdays in the Library of the Zurich Technical University to read recent publications in my field of research. This gave me the extra oxygen I needed to survive.

Everything seemed to be going smoothly and I had bought several books in finance by this time to make sure I will not be outsmarted by the traders with their jargon. But had I spent a few years in the bank, I would have known that nothing goes smoothly in the investment banking world. So, when my colleague informed me that the head of the trading floor wanted to meet with the team, I thought this was perhaps a regular meeting to inform us about business plans.

As I entered the meeting room, a smiling young man with a boyish face like mine greeted us. I was told that he is the head of the trading floor. But I noticed that my boss was missing. After expressing his admiration for the teams' intellectual capacity, he announced that the team has to be reorganised as our boss does not work for the bank any more. But he assured us that we need not worry as every one of us will be accommodated and they have worked out a tentative plan.

The few visits I made earlier to the trading floor and the familiarity with the bond option pricing model secured me a place in the trading floor next to bond traders. I was given a desk at the very end of the trading room from where I had a spectacular view of the Alps on a clear day. An empty desk next to me separated me from the trader, and I was pleased to have this buffer zone. I was told that I had a few months' time to work with the traders and demonstrate to them how I could be useful.

It did not sound reassuring. Work with traders? When do they have the time to talk to me? Why should they care to talk to me if they know how to price and hedge their option trades? I decided to ignore these questions so that I do not get depressed. But I got a helping hand and encouragement from another colleague who had been working for about a year with the traders. He had studied physics, and being Swiss, he was well-networked with the traders. I got some tips as what might be useful pricing tools to develop and he showed me some tricks for getting real time pricing feeds into my spread sheets.

Early morning before the trading started was the best time to talk to traders. I made sure I arrived before they did to engage in small talk with them and to also find out what kinds of option pricing tools might interest them. They were sympathetic and gave some tips what I should focus on. My turn around time was very short, which surprised them. Within a matter of two months I had a portfolio of bond and swap option pricing tools implemented. Occasionally I received requests from traders to check what my pricing model would suggest for a particular trade that was either off-market or illiquid. I realised later that they were testing if my models were any good as they already had quotes from other dealers. They were surprised with the accuracy of my pricing model. In cases where there were price discrepancies, they said that they did not agree with the prices quoted by other dealers.

With the traders happy to communicate with me, I was told that I will be permanently assigned to this bond trading section. It was great relief. The following months the demand for my price quotes and hedging parameter estimates increased. I had implemented by then American and European call and put options, caps, floors, swaptions, forward start options, knock-in and knock-out options, and digital options. Word soon spread in the trading floor that there was a quant who can price anything.

Despite encountering friendly faces everywhere and even managing to hold small talk with traders near the vending machines, there was a sense of unease. Once in a while some traders around me disappeared and I was later told they were fired as they exceeded the loss limits. But there was always a flow of new traders to take their places.

My interactions with traders were brief and focused. They wanted a price for some option, and it was my task to provide them with the price as quickly as possible. No one ever questioned me how I came up with the price and whether I think there could be a margin of error in my estimate. In turn, I never questioned them why they wanted to trade that option and with whom they were trading. That was not my job. I simply had to trust them, and they knew what they were doing. The banking business is after all built on mutual trust. It is a cooperative game with interest of all parties aligned to a common goal – that of making money for themselves, their clients and the institutions they worked for. In such cooperative games there can be no misalignment of interests among parties. We were in a win-win situation.

As in any closed working environment comprising 80 to 100 people with strong egos and struggle for survival, there is going to be jokes and jealousy. But it was the nicknames given to some traders that impressed me most. There was the con-man who could come up with convincing rumours about any topic that his client had interest in for creating the opportunity to enter into a profitable trade. The cook, referring to an equity trader who had training as a cook, had a great sense of smell to spot the best stocks. The stunt-man displayed his acrobatic skills by talking to three clients at the same time over the phone while holding three receivers.

There were others too. The "fach-idiot," a German word referring to someone who only knows his subject of study, was an extremely bright German mathematician who irritated the traders by asking many technical questions that no one understood. And there was the hated economist whose job was to provide interpretation over the speaker of the possible market reactions when economic releases or policy decisions were communicated. All traders closed their ears when he spoke. They told me that his assessments would have value if he was either consistently wrong or consistently right. Unfortunately, he was wrong 50 percent of the time which confused traders, and therefore they did not want to listen to his views. Anyway, they said they had no confidence in economists' ability to understand developments in financial markets.

The trading floor was always a very noisy place and I had to remain extremely focused to ensure that I did not make mistakes while programming. But sometimes there was a brief pause in the noise level. I knew immediately that the head of the investment banking division was on the trading floor. It was like the tiger being on the prowl. He had the strange habit of coming and occupying the empty chair next to me. He used to spend five and sometimes ten minutes looking around to get a sense of what is happening on the trading floor. Often he called some traders and asked questions on market developments. On some occasions he even used to stare at my computer screen being puzzled what I am doing there all day long.

These visits happened regularly, almost once a week. He may have taken his seat next to me at least on 20 occasions, but we never said hello, smiled or greeted each other. I did not know what to talk to him and he didn't either. It looked like silence was the best outcome for both of us. After the first few sittings, I asked the trader close to me who this gentleman is and why the noise level fell when he came.

"He is Ossi, the head of investment banking," replied the trader. "No one wants to mess with Ossi. So everyone is careful about what they say when he is around." Ossi was the nickname of Oswald Gruebel who later became the head of Credit Suisse, and subsequently after his retirement, was recalled to lead UBS during the financial crisis.

By the summer of 1995 I had become a trusted partner on the trading floor. I even had the time and courage to enquire about the hobbies of traders if I had a chance to meet them at lunch. Those occasions were rare as traders preferred to eat sandwiches by their desk to stay focused on market developments. It was now already fall season, and there was less than three months to go for Christmas. I was just having lunch with a trader who mentioned that he considers buying a digital option the bank had just announced. They always came up with some product before Christmas, more in the spirit of Santa Claus.

That conversation surprised me as I was often consulted on the pricing of exotic options. I sought more clarification about the option, just being curious. "Well you see, the option has a payoff of SFr 10 if the Libor fixing on 20 December is below 2 percent. If it is above this value you get nothing. The trader managing this product is charging SFr 1 to trade it."

"Are there restrictions as to who can buy this option?" I asked him. "Anyone in Switzerland including you can buy this," he said creating some interest in me.

When I went back to my desk, I had homework to do. I downloaded all the relevant data quickly and checked the prices of other options traded in the market on the same underlying variable, namely the three month Libor fixing. The evolution of the short-term interest rate model I had implemented for pricing bond options was already available. I knew where to dig the trench for drunkards that I had discussed earlier for pricing this option and to estimate the probability of this event happening. The model parameters had to be calibrated to the Swiss interest rate curve using prices of certain types of instruments called caps and floors. All this involved a few hours of work.

The results of my exercise completely surprised me. My model was suggesting the fair price of this option should be around SFr 3. Such a price discrepancy, amounting to more than SFr 2 compared to what the trader was quoting, creates a perfect arbitrage opportunity. As a trader, you can open a position and then close it in a few weeks' time when market forces necessitate a price adjustment to the fair value. Of course, it is always contentious as to what the fair value is. But I trusted my model, and it was saying that there is a 30 percent chance that the 3-month Libor fixing will be below 2 percent before Christmas.

Should I buy? How much should I buy? Well, that depended on how much I am willing to lose. Perhaps I can live with a loss of SFr 1000? It sounded like an astronomical figure to lose. I could have managed to live with that money for three months in Berlin. My wife could have bought all the equipment for the kitchen with that money when she comes over to join me in Zurich after completing her studies. I now slowly started understanding the mental agony a trader would have to go through when they take positions that could end up losing a million dollars.

Over the next quarter of an hour I could not take my mind off this trade. After all it is bad experience that teaches good lessons.

Finally, mustering enough courage I went to the trader offering this product to customers. "I came to know you are offering a digital option that gives you a payoff of SFr 10 if the Swiss 3-month rate is below 2 percent. Can I buy some of this option?"

The trader did not want to take me seriously. They all knew me as being extremely risk averse even when it comes to betting the bank money. "Do you want to show me that you have trader instincts in addition to your quant skills?"

But suddenly he became inquisitive. He knew there could be something wrong in the pricing. "How much will you be willing to pay for this option?" he asked me. "At three francs I would not be buying this option as that is the fair price," I replied.

The trader was not amused as he knew the prices I came up with for many trades were known to be accurate. "Are you using the funny model you implemented to come up with this price?" he asked me.

"Yes, it is based on the one-factor Hull and White model and calibrated to current prices of caps and floors," I told him. "How did you come up with your price?"

"Why, I used Bloomberg as usual," he said. "Moreover, my gut feeling tells me that there is no way the 3-month Libor fixing will fall 75 basis points over the next two months."

What he was saying is that he has seen historical patterns of how fast this rate had changed, and with the current Libor rate at

2.75 percent, he sees very low probability of the rate falling below 2 percent to trigger a SFr 10 payment. His subjective assessment of the event probability was less than 10 percent, and this justified him to charge SFr 1 for the option.

"You must have used the Black-Scholes model in Bloomberg," I argued. "That is a wrong model to use for interest rate options."

"But it works. And that is what matters in trading." He had suddenly lost faith in my funny model.

I did not want to have further arguments with him. I just had to trust his intuition and skills. He had been in this business much longer. Before I left, I gave him my securities account that I had just opened and asked him to buy 1000 contracts worth one franc each for receiving a SFr 10 as payoff on each of these contracts if the option conditionality is met at expiry.

Word spread the next day on the trading floor that I had bought this Christmas option. Many traders were sure that I had done my homework. I came to know later that some of them also decided to buy this option. By late afternoon the next day, another large investment bank in Zurich offered to buy the entire lot of this option on offer. The trader had raised the price already after my intervention to SFr 1.5 to play it safe. But it seemed not sufficient. After trading with the rival bank, there were no more Christmas options on offer. In a few days' time, the rival bank was willing to sell back some of the options it bought for SFr 3. I saw this opportunity and closed my position to make a profit of SFr 2000 in less than a week.

I received a call soon from the head of the trading floor to meet him. The trader had related the conversation he had with me earlier. "You should not have bought the option," the head of the trading floor told me.

"But I got the consent of the trader before I bought it," I contested.

"He has no authority on these matters," he said. "But since it was a small amount, I am not concerned. Your job is to cooperate with traders, not to compete with them."

This anecdote is not meant to exemplify a profitable trade I did once in my life. Rather, it is meant to illustrate how traders operate and how their beliefs and subjective probability assessments influence their position taking. While some pricing models may be used as a supporting tool, most risk taking in the financial markets are driven by beliefs and a sense of what might be a good timing to implement those views using financial instruments that are best suited for holding such risk exposures. There is more of a behavioural element than rational choice in financial decision making. Luck, destiny and your astrological signs determine outcomes.

The use of financial modelling tools is more suited for managing risk. That is, to assess how far away our drunkard, if we treat him as our financial variable, will find himself from his house when he returns from the pub. He could find himself on either side of the house. But that information is not of much help as the trader has to bet whether the drunkard will find himself to the right or to the left of his house to make money. To figure this out the trader may have to eavesdrop on what the drunkard is telling his friend at the bar. If he hears him say after several beers that he is going to sleep with his girlfriend that night who lives 10 houses to the left because his wife will throw him out when he returns so drunk, there is a good chance that the drunkard will end up on the left side of his house. That is the kind of information traders are looking for to place their bets.

There were other lessons I learned working in Zurich. One day as I was preparing to leave as my working day ended, a trader came to me and said that one of the big pharmaceutical clients in Switzerland wanted to enter into a large sized option trade. This was a digital option contract they wanted to enter into on their own stock, and the size of the position and the nature of payoff would mean it will be difficult to hedge the exposure. The pharmaceutical client had an in-house expert who had calculated the price of this option, and they wanted to have the traders' quote. As is often the standard practice, the trader had tried to compute the price of this option using the pricing tools in Bloomberg, and the option price was very similar to the one the client was expecting.

The trader was convinced that it was a wrong price, and there was no way he could enter into this trade. Being an important client, he simply could not ignore their request. He now needed my help to come up with a price significantly higher, and then provide good arguments for the same. The trader already had a guess of what that price should be.

I knew this was not going to be simple. The historical volatility of the returns on the stock was not high, and even if I raised it by 5 percentage points, the price of the digital option was only marginally higher. But I suddenly came up with this idea of a drunkard heading to his girlfriend rather than to his wife. As the girlfriend's house is closer to the where the trenches are, the probability that the drunkard will fall into the trench is significantly higher. Those higher probabilities translate to higher option price.

Indeed, I figured out that the returns on this stock over the previous two years had been significantly high. Periods of high returns turn out to be periods of low volatility in stock markets. The problem with option pricing models is that they assume the expected return on the stock will be the same as that of the risk-free rate or simply the bank deposit rate. That rate was 2 percent per annum. But against the backdrop of the performance of the stock market and of this stock in particular, this expected return assumption posed some problems. When I raised this rate of return to 5 percent to reflect the market expectations at that time, I got a price close to where the traders' intuition told him it should be. I gave this price to him and explained how I arrived at the price.

"Our in-house quant has priced this option," the trader told his client. "The price is three times higher, and the underlying assumption is that the expected return on the stock is 5 percent based on current market expectations rather than the risk-free rate of 2 percent." The trade was not executed and I felt relieved that I could go home.

While demands on my time had increased, my interest in what I was doing waned. I knew I could write programs to price more complex options or implement other interest rate models. Yet, I did not grasp the bigger picture of the banking business I was now part of. I struggled to understand what purpose was being served by offering these options to economic agents. It was also not clear to me what I would be doing in two years' time other than pricing more options and keeping a record of the average life span of traders on the floor before being fired.

Sometime in early 1996 I was requested to help the risk management division with questions on appropriate models to use for market risk measurement. There were new rules under the Basel regulation to estimate and report capital requirements for market risk. I was told that this was based on a concept called value at risk. That took me off on a tangential path as I tried to learn what value at risk meant. This kept me busy and interested.

Already by this time I was exploring other opportunities. One came up in Frankfurt that looked promising as it would involve less interaction with traders. But they offered me a salary that was less than 60 percent of what I was earning. When I drew their attention to this, the hiring manager explained that I would be making much more money than working in India. But I was not working in India. When he called me again a week later to check if I had changed my mind, I told him that I did and I have decided to live and work in Switzerland.

While being preoccupied with value at risk documents, I discovered an advertisement from the institution behind this new regulation. The name of that institution was Bank for International Settlements, and I recalled a reference to this name in the value at risk document I was reading. But that technical document was prepared by JP Morgan and not the Bank for International Settlements. So I was not sure what this new bank I had discovered was doing. I always knew that I can find out when the time comes. For now they were looking for someone who can price bond options and also can work with traders managing government bond portfolios. I had been to the city of Basel and I knew German was being spoken there, which made it sound attractive in a multi-lingual Switzerland.

I was delighted to be called for an interview. The lady in the Human Resources assured me that it is very easy to find the bank, which happens to be a tall building that I will see as I walk out of the railway station. When I came out of the railway station, I was looking for a large sign board with the name Bank for International Settlements. As I did not see this, I walked past this tall building. The next one was the Hilton hotel that I immediately recognised. I was now confused. I asked a few people on the side walk if they knew where this Bank for International Settlements is. They did not have a clue, but suggested that there are big banks a few minutes down the road.

I was glad to see a bank at the end of the road, but this was UBS, a large Swiss bank. I was confident that people here should know where the other bank I was looking for is located. When I enquired at the reception, the lady was perplexed. She has not heard of this Bank for International Settlements she told me. After enquiring the address of the bank, she said it must be somewhere close to the railway station. I went back and this time decided to enquire at the strange looking tall building I had passed. I had failed to take note of small sign on the wall that had the name of the bank engraved. To my relief, the man at the reception confirmed I was at the right bank.

The interview turned out to be very friendly. Three of the five people who interviewed me were Germans and the others Belgians. I knew from my trading floor experience that I need to keep out all mathematical jargon as bankers do not understand this. My fluency in German impressed them and they were confident I will have no problem to adjust to a lifestyle in Basel. Having worked in a major Swiss bank, they felt my technical skills do not have to be tested. In a few weeks after that I received the job offer to join in June 1996.

In Zurich, I announced to the traders that I will be leaving to work at the Bank for International Settlements in Basel. "Bank for what?" asked a trader. "I have never heard of such a bank, and I have been in this business for ten years."

Many traders were inquisitive and wanted to know what business this bank was doing. I could not say much either, but I assured them that such a bank existed and that I had been there a month back. The traders and other colleagues wished me good luck in my new career in the strange bank I decided to work for.

CHAPTER THREE

DISCOVERING BASEL

The city of Basel lies in north-western Switzerland on the river Rhine. An important event in the development of the city was the founding of the Basel University in the year 1460, the oldest in Switzerland. Some of the great mathematicians of the 17th and 18th century, such as Jakob Bernoulli, Johann Bernoulli, Daniel Bernoulli and Leonhard Euler taught in Basel. During the same period and even extending into the 19th century, silk weaving, textile manufacturing and dyeing industries flourished given the ample supply of water from the river Rhine. This gave rise subsequently to today's chemical and pharmaceutical companies that dominate the landscape of Basel. It is in one of the Basel pharmaceutical companies, the Sandoz Laboratories, that the drug LSD was first synthesized by a Swiss chemist in 1938.

This city now hosts the oldest international financial institution, the Bank for International Settlements, which is better known as the BIS. It was established in 1930 pursuant to an international treaty with the purpose of facilitating reparations imposed on Germany by the Treaty of Versailles after World War I. The Bank's name is derived from this original role. As a consequence of the Great Depression of the 1930s as well as developments in Germany after that, the reparations issue quickly faded. Subsequently, when the Second World War ended, the establishment of the International Monetary Fund and the World Bank created an existential threat to BIS. It survived this threat due to the intervention of John Maynard Keynes in support of the BIS. With the reparations issue out of the way, the BIS focused its activities on technical cooperation between central banks in the areas of reserve management, foreign exchange transactions, gold deposit and swap facilities, and in providing a forum for regular meetings of central bank Governors and officials.

As I found myself now working for this international organisation with a long history, I tried to find out more about its mandate and my role in the organisation. I was generally happy that life was not so fast paced as on the trading floor of an investment bank, and that my colleagues had time to engage in intellectual small talk. Often, they were the young economists from the Monetary and Economics Department who were also glad to learn more about financial markets. I enjoyed these discussions and was pleased to have found a middle ground between university life and banking industry. During one of those discussions, the head of the monetary policy section, Stefan, recommended that I should try to learn more economics. He was just starting to teach a course on monetary policy at the Basel University and I could attend he said. The insights I got into the Mundell-Fleming model, the transmission channels of monetary policy and the Phillips curve from the lectures helped me in my communication with economists.

At my new work place I noticed that no one was being in a great hurry, and therefore, I had to take some initiative to find out what my deliverables are going to be. I discovered that the portfolio managers that I was to work with were not trading in options and other derivatives. That did not disappoint me as there were other interesting things to learn here. Indeed, it was during the many years that I spent in the banking department of the BIS that I managed to make the full transition from being an engineer to becoming a banking expert. At the same time I also managed to uncover many facts about BIS and its influential role in the design of international banking regulation.

For a significant part of the second half of the 20th century, the BIS was better known among the member central banks it served as a provider of banking services. Given the character of its establishment, the BIS was seen mainly as a forum for cooperation among European central banks with the United States playing a limited role until the early 1990s. During the 1960s the BIS played an important role in coordinating the response of the central banks to the challenge of keeping the Bretton Woods system of fixed exchanges rates running smoothly. This required significant amount of banking operations to be performed, including the creation of a common gold pool to intervene in private gold markets as well as the creation of a currency swap network for central banks. The expertise gained through these operations allowed BIS to offer services to central banks in the gold and foreign exchange markets and also to provide liquidity in the reserve currencies by accepting deposits that were redeemable. These operations helped the BIS to be self-financed without government budgetary support unlike the Bretton Woods institutions. This provided great independence in determining the activities BIS could pursue with central banks without any political interference.

But many changes to the composition and character of its mandate were already being contemplated under the stewardship of Andrew Crockett when he became the General Manager in 1994. Change creates opportunities for newcomers like me, but uncertainties for long-serving employees, and I could sense the displeasure among some when I joined the BIS. Andrew Crockett was convinced that the BIS has to reinvent itself and stop being a Europe-focused institution considering that the European Central Bank (ECB) was to go into operation very soon. He wanted to see more faces like mine at the institution to give it an international flavour.

Under Crockett's leadership, the Governors of the central banks of Canada, Japan and the United States joined the BIS Board of Directors, and aligned Board membership with membership of the G10. Prior to this, Board members were the Governors of the central banks of Belgium, France, Germany, Italy, the Netherlands, Sweden, Switzerland and the United Kingdom. In 1996 the central banks of Brazil, China, Hong Kong, India, Korea, Mexico, Russia, Saudi Arabia and Singapore were invited to become shareholders to make the BIS a truly international institution. Private investors holding the BIS shares were forced to sell their shares back to the BIS in 2001, and shareholding rights were restricted subsequently to only central banks. In 2016, the BIS had sixty shareholding central banks.

It was a great privilege to be in the midst of the transformation process of an institution from being Europe-focused to becoming truly global. From the perspective of the banking department I worked for, this transformation created greater demands for financial services from the new shareholding central banks. That involved broadening the product range offered by the BIS to central bank customers, but was soon followed by requests for supporting their efforts to strengthen risk and reserve management practices. I had a role to play in both.

Not many outside the central banking community know much about the financial services BIS offers central banks and other official institutions. In fact, many BIS employees, excluding those working for the banking department or the risk management section, are still not aware of the financial services offered by the institution. Since 1998, the banking department is located in a different building, called the Botta after the architect who constructed it, from the main BIS building, called the Tower. The information on activities performed in Botta is seldom shared with the Tower beyond those at the senior management level. This is because of the confidentiality of the financial transactions that the BIS sometimes performs in currency and gold markets on behalf of central banks.

The banking department of the BIS performs activities that are very similar to that of a normal bank. But it only acts as a bank for customers that are either central banks or certain other official institutions. As any bank, it takes deposits from its customers that are denominated in one of the major reserve currencies. It also executes foreign exchange transactions, which could be a currency intervention on behalf of a central bank, and handles gold sales and other related transactions in the gold market. The broadening of the shareholder base in 1996 led to an increased demand from the new member central banks for BIS instruments that allowed funds placement beyond one year maturity. There was also desire among some central banks to outsource to the BIS the management of a small portion of their government bond portfolio.

The activities of the BIS are financed exclusively by the revenues generated from the financial services offered by the banking department. The BIS also holds a sizeable amount of gold reserves although they are not revenue generating. But the lion's share of the shareholder equity, which is more than USD 25 billion as of 2016, is held in government bonds. Interest income from investing the own funds of the BIS in government bonds and the net interest margins earned on deposits made by central banks provide the revenues for conducting the BIS activities.

I was assigned to the team entrusted with managing the own funds of the BIS in government bonds. My specific task was to help construct appropriate benchmarks against which the performance of these bond portfolios will be measured, and to build tools to monitor and manage those risks. Building those tools helped me gain great insight into the operations of the asset management industry, which is distinct from the investment banking I had seen earlier.

From the perspective of the managers of those portfolios, they wanted tools for measuring the excess returns, if any, that they managed to generate during a given month. And more importantly, to attribute those excess returns to exposures to various risk factors they had taken. The outcome of the exercise was to show that those excess returns were generated by portfolio manager skills to predict market movements. Any other conclusion drawn from the risk and performance attribution model would result in questioning the validity of the model.

For many, the term risk model would sound like Latin words. The inner workings of the risk model were certainly Latin words for most people working in the banking department. But as I mentioned earlier, and I will repeat this often, the banking business is built on trust. And everyone in the banking department trusted me. They even agreed to communicate the risk measures generated by the model I helped implement to central banks that had given the portfolio management mandate. But what is a risk model and how does the asset management industry use it for its daily operations? Let me provide some insights on this.

As an investor, if we give money to a wealth manager, we have to specify how that money has to be invested. Should it be invested in equities, bonds or a combination of both? If it were to be in equities, should it be invested in S&P 500, the German DAX or the Japanese Nikkei index? Assuming the choice is S&P 500, can the manager have the discretion to deviate from the relative weights of the different shares in the index? Would shares other than those in the index be permitted to be held in the portfolio?

Any investment mandate requires having a formal agreement on the answers to the above questions. What it tells us is that there is a need for some agreed benchmark against which the performance of the investment manager will be measured, and some mechanism to quantify the risks arising from investment deviations from the agreed benchmark. In a nutshell, the asset management industry focuses on relative measures of performance and risk versus some benchmark. Those relative measures are derived using a construct called factor models.

A factor is simply some attribute that can be used to explain an event. We are often used to attributing different factors for our own success or failure in some endeavour. If we can collect the list of all factors that can influence the success or failure of an outcome, say of a Presidential race, we can speak of a having built a factor model to explain the results. The premise in financial economics is that returns on market securities can be associated with different attributes. For equities, those attributes can be divided into yield, book-to-market ratio, industry membership, and others. These attributes are called fundamental factors. For bonds, one can use inflation expectations, growth and creditworthiness of the issuer as attributes. The first two of these attributes would fall under the category of macroeconomic factors. But the attributes or factors can also be derived by examining the statistical relationships embedded in past returns across different securities.

Building a risk model translates to identifying the relevant common factors that can collectively explain the sources of returns on different securities. The statistical relationship between these factors, which goes by the technical term covariance matrix, constitutes the risk model. The differences in relative exposures to these factors held by the asset manager between the benchmark and the portfolio helps to pin point the sources of risk. Out- or underperformance versus the benchmark can then be attributed the choices made by the asset manager to underweight or overweight exposures to certain risk factors that drive returns.

The risk model for a bond portfolio, for example, can be constructed using the changes in the shape of the yield curve as factors. For example, the yield curve can move up or down, meaning a level shift. This level shift would then represent one factor in the risk model. The yield curve could also steepen or flatten. A steepening of the yield curve would imply that the medium and long term rates rise more than the short term rate. This steepening or flattening of the yield curve can be used to represent the second factor in the risk model. A change in the shape of the yield curve would translate to a change in the price of the bond held in the portfolio. If the investment universe includes both US government bonds and Japanese government bonds, we would have to include two additional risk factors to represent the movements of the Japanese yield curve. Changes in the US dollar versus Japanese yen exchange rate would have to be also included resulting in a five factor risk model in this case.

The theory sounds quite simple but one encounters a number of practical difficulties when doing the risk attribution. The difficulties stem from the market liquidity of the securities held in the portfolio. For an equity portfolio, the liquidity-related problems are inconsequential unless the benchmark to be replicated comprises thinly traded equities in less developed economies.

For bond portfolios, the liquidity factor tends to play an important role even with an issuer of bonds with good credit ratings. This is because highly rated non-government bonds, such as triple-A rated corporate bonds, are likely to be bought and held to maturity by institutional investors. Often, there is very little of freely tradable bonds of this category. These bonds may not be traded for several days and the estimate of the prices of these bonds provided by the data vendor for valuation and risk management purposes will not reflect the quotes where traders will take orders. Price quotes on lower rated bonds face similar problems. What the data vendor does in cases where bonds are not traded regularly is to estimate their price based on other bonds with similar features that were traded. In the market jargon, this is called matrix pricing. These prices can sometimes grossly misrepresent the liquidation value of a bond that is held in the portfolio. In fact, the mispricing of the liquidation value of high-grade illiquid complex securitisation products by a large margin of error was a significant factor that contributed to the financial crisis.

But why is poor market liquidity of the securities held in a portfolio problematic? That is because risk quantification models require an estimate of past changes in prices. When prices do not change simply because the underlying securities did not trade, the risk model would forecast that there is no risk or very little risk in the portfolio being held. These problems do not arise in actively traded markets, such as in highly rated government bond markets. But when the managers are allowed to hold less liquid non-government bonds in their portfolio, risks of their holdings tend to be underestimated.

From the perspective of an asset manager, this is not a problem. On the contrary, they would welcome this underestimation of risk. When the coupons paid on some of the less liquid securities held in the portfolio are higher than the average coupon of the benchmark, a small excess return is generated every month. Effectively, this means that the manager is able to outperform his benchmark without taking any risk or taking only very little risk. The market jargon is that the manager's investment strategy generates alpha and has a high information ratio. The investment management industry crowns them as kings of finance.

The experiences I gained from implementing the risk management tools opened new frontiers. This period, between 1996 and 1999, was tumultuous for central banks. Latin America was emerging from the Mexican peso crisis while Asia, and subsequently Russia, entered into crisis mode. They manifested as currency crisis with the foreign reserves management department of central banks playing an active role during the crisis response. At the same time, a major change in the reserves currency composition took place with the introduction of the euro in 1999. The central banks that became new shareholders of the BIS were looking for a trusted partner to coordinate and share experiences on managing foreign exchange reserves and the related risk management practices.

A pervasive theme during the bilateral meetings and seminars held with reserves managers was what constitutes adequate level of foreign exchange reserves. The desire to build up a war chest of reserves to ward-off potential currency attacks was intense. The conditionalities that came with the IMF bailout made Asian countries determined not to seek IMF assistance once more. The bilateral swap arrangements among central banks in Asia under the Chiang Mai initiative in 2000 to meet short-term liquidity needs was one response to build better safeguards. But accumulating foreign currency reserves was seen as the main pillar of support to resist future currency attacks. I recall the great joy and pride that reserves managers had when they announced that their central banks has crossed the $100 billion mark in currency reserves. Foreign currency reserves rose from $1.6 trillion in 1999 to $4.3 trillion in 2005.

I witnessed two specific developments in the period 1999 to 2005 that affected risk pricing in global markets. Many have reported on this earlier. The first was a shift away from investing foreign currency reserves in short-term instruments. This was done by creating a second tranche called the investment portfolio that allowed foreign currency reserves to be invested in medium and long term bonds. The second was to adopt portfolio management concepts and using government bond benchmarks for measuring the risk and performance of the investment portfolio. For reserves held in euros, this meant the replication of government benchmarks that included bonds issued by all euro area countries. In the US Treasuries market, this shift in reserve management strategy together with other factors, such as lower inflation expectations and perhaps also forecasts of lower growth, pushed long-term bond yields lower. In the euro area, the reserve management strategies contributed on top of other developments to compress the relative interest rate spreads between various government bond markets.

My own takeaway while working closely with central bank reserve management departments around the world was that the investment decisions of reserve managers had a more profound impact on government borrowing rates in the medium and long term. The US Treasury announced the retirement of the 30-year maturity bond in this period. At a reserve management seminar for senior central bank officials in the Asia-Pacific region in 2001, a US Treasury official invited to the seminar wanted to know from central banks how their investment strategy will change given the forecast that the Treasury debt will shrink. He was concerned that central banks may not find sufficient quantities of US Treasuries to invest in given the rapid pace of reserves growth. One central banker remarked that they have not taken any policy action as developments at that time were just a passing phenomenon. They were convinced that the Treasury debt supply will rise soon.

This view was shared broadly among Asian central bankers I met then, despite forecasts to the contrary being made from the US official position. But the outstanding amounts of US government notes and bonds provided some backing to the US official position. They amounted to $2.43 trillion in 1999, which then declined to $2.02 trillion in 2001, and subsequently rose to $2.87 trillion in 2005. The new investment flows from central bank foreign currency reserves into US government and government guaranteed securities from 1999 to 2005 amounted about $1.3 trillion and new flows into euro area government securities amounted to about $0.6 trillion. As more investments poured into US government bonds while the outstanding volumes of debt remained stagnant, it had the effect of depressing medium and long-term US interest rates. The behaviour of the US yield curve shape was regarded as a conundrum at that time.

But how do central banks manage to accumulate foreign exchange reserves? When a country exports more goods than what it imports, the surplus revenues generated by international trade is one channel through which foreign exchange reserves can accumulate. The central bank can regulate these foreign currency earnings by retaining it on its balance sheet, and in return, issue short-term debt instruments in the domestic currency to the bank that acts as the intermediary to the company. This is usually the case when the current account is not liberalised.

In developed economies, the free convertibility of the domestic currency, the absence of restrictions on foreign currency transfers, and well-developed domestic capital markets will allow the companies and individuals to manage the net foreign currency revenues. This would be the case, for example, in Germany, Japan or Switzerland. But even in such countries, some of the surplus foreign currency flows could be absorbed directly into the central bank balance sheet against selling the domestic currency to intermediating banks. This would also contribute to reserves accumulation.

Another channel through which reserve currency accumulation occurs is when a central bank explicitly intervenes in the foreign exchange market to maintain the export competitiveness of the economy. Such interventions can happen even if there is a trade deficit. Acquiring foreign currencies by selling domestic currency debt instruments to banks would allow a central bank to dampen any appreciation pressures that might confront the domestic currency.

But why would a central bank want to invest its foreign currency investments in long-term bonds that increase interest rate risk on its balance sheet? The short answer to the question is that the accounting conventions used by central banks are different from those of private sector enterprises. It is usually based on accrual accounting with financial instruments acquired being held at purchase price and profits being recognised in the profit and loss statement only upon sale or maturity of the instrument. Therefore, increasing the maturity of the instruments held on the balance sheet does not translate into greater fluctuations in the central banks' reported profits.

The compelling argument for a central bank to increase the maturity of its bond holdings comes from its role in contributing to the revenues of the state. Many central banks in emerging economies even enter into an advance arrangement with their governments as to the profits they will transfer at the end of the financial year, which is usually subject to a mid-term revision. Extending the maturity of investments on its reserves portfolio allows a central bank to increase the interest income when the yield curve is upward sloping. This gives a boost to the revenues it can transfer to the government. Indeed, it became common practice among central banks at that time to create two tranches, one called the liquidity and the other the investment tranche. Buying medium- and long-term foreign currency bonds in the investment tranche allowed emerging market central banks to raise its profit transfers to the government.

A word of caution may be warranted here. The purchase of bonds by many advanced economy central banks under the name quantitative easing does not constitute reserve currency accumulation. Such bonds denominated in the domestic currency of the central bank can be acquired without incurring any foreign exchange risk. The motives for purchasing bonds under the quantitative easing program are very different from reserve currency accumulation. But it also affects the shape of the medium- and long-term part of the yield curve, and this impact is an explicit objective of the quantitative easing program. While this yield curve shape shift is being engineered by advanced economy central banks in the post crisis period, during the pre-crisis period the same effects that happened through reserve currency accumulation have been argued to have had destabilising effects on financial markets.

The implications of the collective decisions of various market participants on the stability of the financial system became a recurring theme in policy debates taking place in the BIS meetings. There was a need to improve banking supervisors' skills as more countries started adopting Basel regulation for banks. The BIS and the Basel Committee on Banking Supervision jointly created the Financial Stability Institute (FSI) in 1999 to assist financial sector supervisors around the world in improving and strengthening their financial systems.

At the same time, the lessons drawn from the Asian and Russian financial crisis created a need to have a forum where mechanisms that lead to such financial instabilities can be discussed and policy tools needed to address them formulated. Andrew Crockett, the General Manager of the BIS, did not let such a golden opportunity slip. The Financial Stability Forum (FSF) was founded in 1999 with Andrew Crockett as its first Chairman to promote international cooperation on financial stability. The Secretariat of the committee was located at the BIS. In April 2009 at the G20 Summit, the FSF was transformed into international body under the name Financial Stability Board (FSB) to monitor and make recommendations about the global financial system. The city of Basel has now become the place where global financial rules and regulation are discussed, debated and drafted to create a stronger and more resilient financial architecture.

CHAPTER FOUR

BASEL II

The city of my choice is better known outside Switzerland through the Roman numerals attached to it – Basel I, Basel II or Basel III. It almost sounds like the different versions of software releases of vendors that most of us are familiar with. Indeed, there was a release called Basel 2.5 during the financial crisis making such comparisons relevant.

But what are these different versions of Basel, and whom do they apply to? For many, who never studied banking and finance or worked in the financial services industry, these words may sound strange and are unlikely to trigger much interest. I too did not care much when my attention was drawn to Basel I at the time I joined the BIS. Yet, the rules for banking business specified by these words had profound implications for the financial sector and their risk-taking activities, and through this, on the economic outcomes that affected the common man on the street. I will try to shed some light on Basel I and Basel II. The latter is particularly important as it is an essential prerequisite for understanding structures that created adverse financial incentives allowing stresses in bank balance sheets to build up while keeping them well-concealed.

Any influential committee or important regulation in the financial sector has usually come into force following a deep crisis. The Basel Committee on Banking Supervision responsible for various versions of Basel releases has its origin to the turmoil in foreign exchange markets that followed the breakdown of the Bretton Woods system of managed exchange rates in 1973. The committee's decision, presented in the form of standards of the type

Basel I or II, have no legal force. It publishes these supervisory standards and guidelines with the expectation that individual national authorities will implement them.

But what makes banks so special and different from other companies and non-financial corporations? A simple answer would be that banks can collect deposits from us and the government has to provide some safeguards that we will get our money back. Yet, we also entrust our savings with money market mutual funds and other investment managers who do not comply with similar standards. So, to repeat the question, what is so special about banks?

The distinguishing feature of banks compared to other financial intermediaries is that banks are also entrusted with payments and settlements of financial transactions. Money transfers, executing foreign exchange transactions, and maintaining accounts to receive monthly salary payments, are handled exclusively by banks. Any disruption to these services can bring a sudden halt to the engine of economic growth. To maintain uninterrupted services in these areas, the central bank of a country extends liquidity support to banks through collateralised lending and also offers deposit facilities at the central bank. This is an exclusive privilege enjoyed only by banks.

Banks also serve as the conduits through which a central bank tries to influence terms and conditions of lending to the economy and to reach its targets on inflation. In many countries, more than three-quarters of the lending to the real economy is provided by banks. The soundness of the balance sheet of banks is therefore an important pre-requisite for transmitting the goals of the monetary policy of a central bank, be it to spur or dampen the pace of economic activity. That soundness of bank balance sheet is measured by the adequacy of its capital to withstand unexpected losses.

Back in the 1980s, there was no internationally agreed standards on how this unexpected loss can be measured given the exposures or assets held by banks. Many of the assets held by banks comprise residential or commercial mortgage loans and loans to small and medium sized enterprises. As these loans are not traded, there are no market prices for them. Banks value such held-to-maturity loans at the original price at which they were given, and set aside some provisions to cover expected losses based on the riskiness of the borrower using their lending experience. These are called loan loss provisions. The impetus to create a level playing field for internationally active banks on how balance sheet risks should be measured gained momentum during the Latin American debt crisis in the early 1980s.

Before discussing Basel standards, it is useful to understand why monitoring or assessing the balance sheet strengths of non-financial corporations in contrast to banks is much simpler. A typical non-financial corporate will have on its liability side of the balance sheet loans from banks, debt issued, shareholder equity, retained earnings and accounts payable. On the asset side, the balance sheet items include cash reserves, inventory of goods, plant and equipment, and accounts receivable. As sales proceeds fall, cash reserves get depleted and accounts receivable also decline. This will show up as a corresponding reduction in shareholder equity as this is the residual value of the firm after deducting the outstanding loans and debt. Because of this, there is little ambiguity in assessing the balance sheet strength of a non-financial corporate, which is its net worth to shareholders.

The approach taken by banking supervisors until the late 1980s to assess the strength of bank balance sheets did not differ much from that used for non-financial corporates. Supervisors simply took the total capital a bank held, which included shareholder equity and loan loss provisions, and divided this by the total assets of the bank to compute a capital adequacy ratio. In the United States, a ratio above 5.5 percent kept supervisors happy. But the Latin American crisis made it clear that holding a government bond issued by a Latin American country carries more risk than holding a US Treasury bond on a banks' balance sheet.

The 1988 Basel Capital Accord, subsequently referred to as Basel I, was meant to include the riskiness of different categories of assets held by banks when assessing their capital adequacy to withstand shocks. There are many similarities between this approach and an agent who examines the risks involved in insuring a parcel you want to ship. If the parcel contains wine glasses, porcelain cups and metal ash trays, the insurance fees should be higher compared to a parcel of the same weight containing only ash trays. In the same way, a supervisor should expect a bank to be insured with more capital when holding government bonds of developing countries compared to US Treasuries. This leads to the concept of risk weighted assets under the Basel I rules.

Taking the example of the insurance agent again, suppose the insurance fees are expressed per one kilogram of shipped goods with wine glasses costing $8, porcelain cups costing $4 and metal ash trays costing $1.6. Upon customer enquiries, the insurance agent may say that the shipping fees are expressed as a percent of the propensity of goods to break while being transported. Items subject to greatest damage will carry a 100 percent fee; items like porcelain will carry 50 percent fee; and metal objects 20 percent of the fee. The highest insurance fee for shipping one kilogram of goods will be $8. This will allow the customer to calculate what it will cost to ship the parcel containing different objects.

The Basel I risk weights are based on this analogy and follows the keep-it-simple principle. Under this standard, government bonds issued by OECD countries carried a zero risk weight. This means that if the bank decides to hold only assets of this category, then the bank did not require any capital to operate. At the other extreme were the loans to enterprises and exposures to corporate bonds, which carried a risk weight of 100 percent. The Basel I rules stipulated that for a $100 loan, banks will have to hold $8 capital if the risk weight is 100 percent. For residential mortgage loans backed by the house as collateral, the risk weight was set to 50 percent. That meant banks needed only $4 of capital to give a $100 mortgage loan. For exposures to banks that were domiciled in OECD countries, the risk weight was set to 20 percent, meaning $1.6 of capital was needed when a bank gave a $100 interbank loan.

Basel I, which required the ratio of capital held to risk-weighted assets to be at least 8 percent, was implemented by many countries in 1992. To illustrate how a bank could be considered to comply with this standard, let us take a bank that holds $100 million in assets which is held entirely as loans to corporates and households. Because the risk weight for these assets is 100 percent, the risk-weighted assets of the bank will amount to $100 million. To meet the minimum capital requirement ratio, the bank will have to hold at least $8 million of capital. Suppose the same bank sells $50 million of its loan portfolio and acquires from the proceeds $50 million of government bonds issued by OECD countries. Considering that the government bonds will have a zero risk weight, the bank would be able to meet its minimum capital ratio of 8 percent by holding only $4 million of capital.

An important milestone achieved under Basel I standard was to get an international agreement on what constitutes bank capital. This led to two types of bank capital instruments to be defined: one being the core or Tier 1 capital; and the other being supplementary or Tier 2 capital. Shareholder equity and retained earnings are treated as Tier 1 capital. The remaining, which include asset revaluation reserves, general loan loss provisions, undisclosed reserves, hybrid capital instruments and subordinated debt instruments count towards Tier 2 capital.

Let me elaborate on some of the categories of capital listed above. Shareholder equity is the amount paid up to purchase the shares of a bank when it was issued. It is not the amount that those shares are trading today in the stock market. Retained earnings are the profits not distributed as dividends to shareholders and are available to absorb losses if they were to occur. General loan loss provisions correspond to money set aside by a bank to cover future losses if they were to occur based on historical loss estimates for similar exposures. Because they are set aside for losses that have not been incurred, banks are allowed to include this in their capital under Tier 2. Good provisioning practices ensure that banks do not report profits upfront that could be distributed as dividends, as general provisions are included in the equity but not in the profit and loss account. Asset revaluation reserves can arise if a bank held assets that have been valued at acquisition price, such as real estate, but decided to revalue them at current market price.

The minimum capital requirement under Basel I took the sum of both Tier 1 and Tier 2 capital instruments and stipulated that this should be at least 8 percent of risk weighted assets. As banks started complying with the new capital standard, the simplicity of the rule already exposed many shortcomings. Basel I essentially dealt with one form of risk, namely credit risk. This is the risk that a counterparty to which the bank has lent money may be unable to repay it. Other forms of risk, such as incurring a loss due to changes in market value of an instrument held to support trading activities, are not included. This would fall under the category of market risk. But even under credit risk, banks do mitigate counterparty or credit risk with other banks arising from interbank transactions by entering into netting agreements on bilateral exposures. Towards end-1995, revised rules were proposed to recognise the effects of bilateral netting agreements to reduce the net asset exposures on which the risk weights were applied.

A significant upgrade to Basel I came in end-1997 with the market risk amendment to the capital accord. This amendment required banks to set aside capital to cover risks from their trading activities involving foreign exchange, equities, debt securities and derivatives products. These activities were more confined to investment banks or large universal banks that supported their clients' buying and selling of financial instruments and products. As these assets were held-for-trading, it was customary to refer to the market risk capital requirement applying to the trading book rather than to the banking book in which held-to-maturity assets were kept. In the regulatory jargon, credit risk capital requirements applied to the banking book.

But how is market risk to be measured? I can recollect very few people involved in the banking business or regulatory community understood the underpinnings of how models used to estimate market risk really worked when it was first introduced. All I can say is that it involved statistical concepts and was developed by engineers working in JP Morgan in the early 1990s. The models they used were made available to the banking community, which the banking supervisors subsequently adopted. Let me provide a bird's eye view of what is involved in the modelling process.

Let us assume that a bank holds $10 million worth of securities in its trading book. As the quoted price of the securities change each day, the value of the securities portfolio held by the bank will also change. For example, the value of the securities held might increase to $10.05 million or decline to $9.9 million the next day. Suppose we examine all such past changes in the value of this securities portfolio over the past 6 months and conclude that on average the value changes by $0.1 million. In statistical terms this price fluctuation or volatility is measured as the standard deviation of price changes. The measure of daily volatility in price changes in this example corresponds to 1 percent. A histogram of these price changes generally tends to closely resemble a bell-shaped curve that has certain characteristic properties. If 1 percent is the average volatility of changes in prices, using the properties of the bell-shaped curve one can say that the daily price changes will not exceed 2.5 percent with a confidence level of 99 percent. This gives rise to the concept of market value-at-risk at 99 percent confidence level.

To determine capital requirements for market risk, the regulatory standard assumes that the bank may take up to 10 trading days to sell their positions. As the horizon extends from 1 day to 10 days, the potential losses under the assumption that the price changes each day are independent can be calculated by multiplying daily changes by square root of 10, which is the number of trading days. So, the market value-at-risk for a 10-day period measured at 99 percent confidence level will be $0.825 million for holding $10 million of securities $(0.825 = 10 \times 2.5\% \times 3.3)$. Basel I requires that this value is further multiplied by a factor of 3 to account for extreme market risk events which may not have been captured in the data over the past 6 months. Taking this multiplier into account, the bank will be required to set aside $2.475 million in capital to meet the minimum capital requirements for the market risk in its trading book.

To take the calculation one step further, let us now take a bank that holds $100 million worth of loans in its banking book and $10 million worth of securities in its trading book. As the risk weights for loans amount to 100 percent, the risk-weighted assets resulting from credit risk will amount to $100 million. In order to be able to sum risk-weighted assets resulting from credit and market risk exposures, the bank will have to multiply the capital requirement for market risk of $2.475 million in the earlier calculation by a factor of 12.5. This number is simply the reciprocal of the 8 percent minimum capital requirement (ie, $12.5 = 1/0.08$). This gives the risk-weighted assets for market risk as $30.9 million. The total risk weighted assets for credit and market risk amount to $130.9 million. If the bank has to meet a minimum capital ratio of 8 percent, then it needs to hold a capital of at least $10.47 million.

What happens if market conditions change and the volatility of daily price changes of the securities portfolio drops from 1 percent to 0.5 percent? In this case, the bank will have to set aside only $1.237 million rather than $2.475 million in capital for market risk. The minimum capital requirement to cover both credit and market risk will be $9.24 million instead of $10.47 million. Banks will be incentivised to employ the unused capital of $1.23 million to take additional risks on their balance sheet to generate more profits.

In a real world example, the securities portfolio held by a bank in its trading book will comprise debt instruments denominated in different currencies, maturities and asset categories. To compute a forward-looking volatility measure of the trading book portfolio, banks will model multiple yield curves and map cash flows of the debt instruments against the appropriate yield curve. Estimating an aggregate measure of the volatility of all these cash flows would require constructing a risk model similar to the one I described in the previous chapter. There is always some risk that markets might manipulate the risk measure by ignoring the liquidity risk element that is integral to market risk. For example, if banks cooperate with each other to trade small lot sizes of illiquid assets to establish relatively constant prices for those assets over many days or weeks, the yield curve for those asset categories will remain relatively constant. As a consequence, the aggregate volatility measure derived from the risk model will underestimate the true risk embedded in the trading book portfolio.

The model used to compute the equivalent risk weighted assets for market risk becomes more complex as the types and complexity of instruments held on the trading book increases. The illustration here to demonstrate how to calculate the risk weighted assets for market risk uses the internal model approach that a bank may use upon supervisory approval. What is important to note here is that as banks start to trade in more complex instruments employing its trading book, banking supervisors will find it difficult to verify whether the corresponding market risk capital charges estimated by a bank are adequate.

During the mid-1990s, banks with large trading operations invested significantly in building in-house models for risk management. Part of that was linked to building internal models for measuring and reporting capital requirements for market risk under the revised Basel I standard. But banks were also working on building internal models for managing credit risk.

As large banks began trading and hedging their credit risk exposures through more sophisticated derivatives products, the central bank community recognised the need for a new capital adequacy framework. With banks being allowed to choose between a standard supervisory model and an internal model for measuring market risk capital, the demands from banks to have the same discretion for measuring credit risk capital became hard to ignore.

When the market risk amendment came into force in end-1997, the Basel Committee realised that the original Basel Accord conceived in 1988 was already ten years old. Moreover, as financial innovation gathered pace, banks started building superior risk models for their own internal allocation of capital across business units supported by significant enhancements to computational power. The standard risk weights under Basel I was also clearly inadequate to capture the credit risks of diverse counterparties. For example, not all banks domiciled in different OECD countries had the same credit risk as foreseen by using the Basel I risk weights. Moreover, towards the late 1990s, and also subsequently, there was the notion that banks themselves may have greater incentives to police each other. At the same time, credit rating agencies were also assessing the risks of banks and issuers of debt securities that provided an independent view of evolving counterparty credit risks.

These considerations led the Basel Committee to issue a proposal for a new capital adequacy framework in June 1999 to replace the existing Basel I standard. This revised framework known as Basel II comprised three pillars as follows.

Pillar 1: Minimum capital requirements that sought to develop and expand the standardised rules set out in the 1988 Accord.

Pillar 2: Supervisory review of an institution's capital adequacy and internal assessment process.

Pillar 3: Effective use of disclosure as a lever to strengthen market discipline and encourage sound banking practice.

The new Basel standard also introduced quantitative limits on the relative share of core and supplementary capital that a bank should hold. Specifically, the amount of Tier 1 capital held had to be greater than Tier 2 capital. While the minimum capital ratio, that is Tier 1 plus Tier 2 capital divided by risk-weighted assets, had to be at least 8 percent, this rule meant that banks were expected to meet the new standard by ensuring that the Tier 1 capital to risk-weighted assets exceeds 4 percent.

The revised framework turned out to be significantly more complex than the original Basel Accord. Consequently, reaching consensus among banking supervisors across different jurisdictions, as well as ensuring that banks have been consulted on the new regulatory rules, took almost 5 years of intensive preparation. The revised capital framework published in June 2004 came to be known as the Basel II standard. Still, many elements of how market risk has to be measured under the trading book were being finalised. It was only in June 2006 that the comprehensive Basel II standard covering all categories of risk – including one for operational risk – was published for supervisory authorities to adopt through legislation in their respective jurisdictions.

Among the three pillars mentioned above, Pillar 2 and Pillar 3 requirements are of a qualitative nature. Pillar 3 in particular was introduced with the aim to encourage market discipline by developing a set of disclosure requirements for the bank that will allow market participants to assess key pieces of information on various risks, and hence, on the capital adequacy of the bank. This was the self-policing element embedded in Basel II standard by requiring banks to be more transparent in communicating their self-assessment of balance sheet risks, and how the bank intends to address them.

The introduction of Pillar 2 was to enable supervisors to have effective dialogue with bank management to assess their awareness of risks being taken and to ascertain what control and oversight mechanisms were in place. The Basel Committee provided guidance on how this review process should be conducted, which was subsequently adopted by members of the Basel Committee. In a nutshell this involved how the dialogue should be structured with bank management to cover elements such as internal corporate governance (risk controls, compliance, and internal audit), the organisation of the institution's business, and how the institution allocates capital against risk. In addition, supervisors were expected to ascertain how banks intended to meet capital and liquidity shortages that might have been revealed by conducting regular stress tests. This review process gave powers to supervisors to raise capital requirements beyond the minimum level when weaknesses in governance arrangements or potential capital shortfalls from stress tests were revealed.

Pillar 1 was the comprehensive quantitative formulation of how banks have to calculate capital requirements for various risks taken on their balance sheet. They included credit, market and operational risks. The methodology for calculating market risk capital did not change much from the 1997 amendment to market risk under Basel I. The operational risk measurement was still evolving as banks continued to build databases for past losses that occurred from operational errors as well as from costs arising from litigation. But it usually comprised only a small part of the bank capital requirement with limited discretion to change it. Specifically, under a method called the standardised approach, operational risk capital requirements were determined as a fixed percent (12 to 18 percent) of the average gross revenue over 3 years of different business lines.

Banks recognised that the game changer was how credit risk capital requirements were measured under the new standard. Basel II provided banks three alternatives – subject to supervisory approval for two of them – as to how risk weighted assets for credit risk on its banking book can be calculated. One was the standardised approach; the other was internal ratings-based approach, which in turn offered banks two alternatives, a foundation and an advanced approach. The Basel II standard also specified how capital requirements for off-balance sheet exposures and securitised products have to be measured. I will try to focus on these elements of Basel II as they are important to understand the channels through which financial crisis materialised while the self-policing and trust supervisors placed on the banking community under Pillar 2 and Pillar 3 completely broke down.

An important change, as I mentioned above, was methods that were available to banks to calculate risk weighted assets for credit risk. This requires some understanding of credit risk models and how risks are quantified. For assets that are held-to-maturity, credit risk is an assessment of the potential loss that a creditor incurs if the counterparty is unable to repay the money that he has borrowed. Banking supervisors require that banks set aside general loan loss provisions that will cover the expected loss on the asset, which could be a retail loan, mortgage loan, corporate bond or any other asset. The losses that exceed this amount, known as unexpected loss, are to be covered by bank capital. A credit risk model can be thought of as providing estimates of these two variables, the expected and unexpected losses.

To illustrate the principles of credit risk modelling, let me again take the example of throwing a dice. Let us assume that the player (lender) pays $3 to the casino (borrower) to play a game of dice. The rule of the game is that the player gets paid the amount in dollars corresponding to the number that shows up. In this case, the player will lose $1 when the number 2 shows up and will lose $2 when the number 1 shows up. With 6 sides of a dice in all, the probability of each side showing up is 1/6. From the lender's perspective, the expected loss he will incur on this game of dice is $0.5 calculated as below.

Expected loss = $1 x 1/6 + $2 x 1/6 = $3/6 = $0.5

Credit risk models work along the same principles. First, an estimate of the probability of default (PD) is required on the asset held by the bank. In the game of dice, there are two out of six outcomes where a loss (default) will occur, in which case PD=1/3. Second, the models require an estimate of the loss given default (LGD). This is the loss if the borrower defaults, and is expressed as a ratio of the loan extended. In the example above, if the player incurs a loss, there is a 50 percent chance (probability 0.5) that it is either $1 or $2 so that the average loss is $1.5. When it is expressed as a ratio of the $3 the player (lender) paid to the casino (borrower), the LGD for the game of dice is 0.5. The exposure amount of the lender, which is the amount he has paid to the borrower, is $3. This amount is referred to as the exposure at default (EAD). To sum up, the formula for computing the expected loss on an asset held by a bank is given by:

Expected loss = EAD x PD x LGD

The second measure of credit risk that requires allocation of capital is the unexpected loss. This is calculated as the fluctuations or standard deviation of the potential loss in value from holding an asset around its expected loss. For the game of dice, the unexpected loss turns out to be $0.76. A credit risk model will provide an explicit formula to compute the unexpected loss as a function of the underlying variables. This is given by:

$$\text{Unexpected loss} = \text{EAD} \times [\text{PD} \times \text{var(LGD)} + \text{LGD}^2 \times \text{PD} \times (1 - \text{PD})]^2$$

Here, var(LGD) is the variance of the loss given default, which is the square of the standard deviation. The details of the formula are not important here. What is important is the principles of credit risk modelling that underpin how capital requirements are calculated for counterparty default risk arising from bank lending. In practice, the capital requirements are calculated to withstand losses that can happen up to a certain confidence level, which is set at 99.9 percent level under the Basel standard. This is usually referred to as the credit value-at-risk to distinguish it from the market value-at-risk. If the shape of the credit loss distribution is known, a scaling factor can be derived for multiplying the unexpected loss with this factor to derive the credit value-at-risk at 99.9 percent confidence level. When lending takes place to more than one counterpart, an additional term called correlation (R) enters into the calculation. Correlation is the propensity of two counterparties to default together.

Returning to the credit risk capital requirements under Pillar 1, the default option for a bank is to use the standardised approach. This uses fixed risk weights for different assets similar to that under Basel I. A key difference, however, is that these risk weights are not anymore linked to the asset category but rather to the external credit rating of the asset, assuming that one is available. For example, if a bank holds a corporate bond whose issuer is rated AAA by a credit rating agency, it will receive a risk weight of 20 percent under Basel II as opposed to 100 percent it would have received under Basel I.

But what is a credit rating, and how are these assigned? Credit ratings are assigned by rating agencies such as Standard & Poor's, Moody's and Fitch Ratings. Most ratings are solicited, that is the issuer makes a request for receiving a credit rating by making available non-public information on their business strategy and expected cash flows to the rating agency for a prescribed fee. The assigned credit rating of an issuer of debt securities is an opinion about the issuer's capacity to meet its financial commitment to make timely repayments of interest and principal due on the outstanding debt. The various rating categories, which are expressed through some combination of alphabets, represent relative risks of an issuers' capacity to repay debt. Even though the credit ratings themselves are not meant to provide an estimate of the probability of default of an issuer during the course of the next one year, historical data made available by credit rating agencies on defaults will allow one to map a credit rating to an average default probability.

Considering that such issuer ratings are independent opinions expressed by a credit rating agency, and are closely watched by market participants, the Basel Committee was willing to use them to assign risk weights to different categories of assets on bank balance sheets. The risk weights based on rating grades were also seen as a more objective criterion compared to those under Basel I. Banks were also supportive of such a transition as it was seen to be both transparent and simple.

Keeping a few details aside, the standardised risk weights to be used under Basel II for various exposures on the basis of the credit rating of the issuer are given in Box 1. Supervisory discretion was allowed to let banks use lower risk weights, typically zero, when the bank held a bond issued by its sovereign denominated in the domestic currency. The risk weights shown in Box 1 are not applicable to securitisation products, and I will discuss this separately.

Box 1: Risk weights under standardised approach						
Credit rating	AAA to AA−	A+ to A−	BBB+ to BBB-	BB+ to B-	Below B−	Un-rated
Sovereign	0%	20%	50%	100%	150%	100%
Banks	20%	50%	50%	100%	150%	50%
Corporates	20%	50%	100%	150%	150%	100%

For retail exposures under standardised approach, three risk weight categories were used: a risk weight of 35 percent if backed by residential mortgages as collateral; a risk weight of 75 percent if there was no collateral backing the loan; and a risk weight of 100 percent for commercial mortgage loans even if backed by the same collateral.

Large banks having significant trading operations preferred to implement the internal ratings-based (IRB) approach. This offered banks two alternatives – the foundation and the advanced approaches. The IRB approach allowed banks to rely on their own estimates of risk components that allow quantification of credit risk to determine capital requirements. I had earlier explained the different variables involved in modelling credit risk (PD, LGD, R, and EAD), but in addition the effective maturity (M) of a loan also enters into the calculation.

The credit risk model I illustrated earlier examined the case of one loan or one exposure. But banks hold large number of exposures across different categories of borrowers. The calculation of credit risk becomes complex and computationally intense for very large portfolios. To overcome this problem, the Basel Committee used an asymptotic approximation formula applicable to large portfolios to derive the risk weighted asset for each exposure held in the portfolio. Depending on the asset class, these formulas differ slightly. For some who may be interested in details, the specific formulas to be used are shown in Box 2.

What I would like to emphasise is banks were now given greater freedom to improve risk management practices with the hope that they will be prudent and conservative in their capital allocation decisions. That said banks which opted to use the foundation IRB approach had the freedom to choose only the probability of default variable, and other variables in Box 2 were set by the supervisory authority. Only banks using the advanced IRB approach were allowed to choose all the model parameters that govern the calculation of the risk weighted assets for credit risk.

Many readers at this stage are likely to think that these changes, which altered how bank capital requirements were calculated, contributed to the financial crisis. Quite to the contrary, these modifications had limited or even no role in triggering the financial crisis. The criticism that was made against the new standards to determine capital requirements was that it made bank lending, and through this the financial system, more procyclical. What it meant was that banks are likely to lower the estimates of the various credit risk variables under the IRB approach during economic expansions that could result in more free capital available for taking additional risks. In economic downturns, prudent banks will increase the credit risk variables, such as probability of default and loss given default, contributing to a capital crunch that will force banks to reduce lending in such periods.

Box 2: Internal ratings-based approach

Sovereign, bank and corporate exposures

Correlation (R) = 0.12 x (1 – EXP(–50 x PD))/(1 – EXP(–50))

$\qquad$ + 0.24 x [1 – (1 – EXP(–50 x PD))/(1 – EXP(–50))]

Maturity adjustment (b) = $(0.11852 - 0.05478 \times LN(PD))^2$

Residential mortgage exposures

Correlation (R) = 0.15

Maturity adjustment (b) = 0

Other retail exposures

Correlation (R) = 0.03 x (1 – EXP(–35 x PD))/(1 – EXP(–35))

$\qquad$ + 0.16 x [1 – EXP(–35 x PD))/(1 – EXP(–35))]

Maturity adjustment (b) = 0

Capital requirement and risk weighted assets

Capital requirement (K) = $[LGD \times N[(1 - R)^{-0.5} \times G(PD)$

$\qquad$ $+ (R/(1 - R)^{0.5} \times G(0.999))] - PD \times LGD]$

$\qquad$ $\times (1 - 1.5 \times b)^{-1} \times (1 + (M - 2.5) \times b)$

Risk weighted assets (RWA) = K x 12.5 x EAD

Footnote

In above equations, EXP denotes the exponential function, LN the natural logarithmic function, N the cumulative normal distribution function, and G the inverse cumulative normal distribution function.

Actions taken by rating agencies will have similar contractionary effects on lending volumes if they downgrade issuer credit ratings in downturns to reflect increased default risk. This tendency towards amplification in lending volumes during economic expansions, and contractions in lending volumes during economic downturns, is the procyclical element of Basel II rules that came under criticism.

The constructs in the Basel II rules, which in my view were the main culprits during the run up to the financial crisis, were the capital treatment of off-balance exposures, securitisation assets, and collateralised transactions. These assets and transactions constituted only a small share of bank assets at the time when the new standards were still in design stage. I will explain here briefly how capital requirements for these transactions were set under Basel II standard and defer the discussion of how banks exploited these rules that led to build up of vulnerabilities in the financial system to the next chapter.

Off-balance sheet exposures arise when a bank provides a credit commitment to a counterpart. This could be a corporate client, a small business enterprise or even an entity sponsored by the bank at an arms' length. In practice these are credit facilities that have not been drawn down by the counterparty. As these exposures are not on the balance sheet of the bank until drawn, they are treated as off-balance sheet items. Banks are still expected to allocate capital for the credit commitments, but are eligible for a discount called the credit conversion factor (CCF). The assigned CCF value is multiplied with the credit commitment to compute the exposure amount that will require capital allocation for credit risk. A 20 percent CCF value would imply that a credit commitment of $100 will be treated as an exposure of $20 to the counterparty.

For the standardised approach, Basel II rules distinguished commitments that are less than one year and those that are more than one year. Commitments less than one year were assigned a 20 percent CCF whereas those greater than one year received a 50 percent CCF. Under the foundation IRB approach, the CCF was set as 75 percent while for the advanced IRB approach banks were allowed to determine the appropriate CCF. But Basel II rules also introduced an additional clause that allowed commitments that are unconditionally cancellable any time by the bank without prior notice to receive a zero CCF.

Moving on to the securitised assets, these are created by pooling together a large portfolio of assets and then providing some forms of credit enhancements to the pool. The pooling of residential mortgage loans by the US mortgage agencies like Fannie Mae or Freddie Mac and then securitising them to create a mortgage-backed securities (MBS) product is an example of a securitised asset. But the underlying pool of assets under Basel II rules could include any of the following: loans, commitments, asset-backed and mortgage-backed securities, corporate bonds, equities, and private equity investments.

Basel II rules provided a generous capital relief to banks that were pooling assets, securitising them, and selling these securitised assets to a third party without any risk retention requirements. A few preconditions had to be met to get this full capital relief from this origination and distribution of securitised assets. They included among others: (a) significant credit risk associated with the securitised exposures has been transferred to third parties; (b) the assets are legally separated from the transferor, such as through true sale of assets; and (c) the transferee is a special purpose vehicle and the holders of the beneficial interests in that vehicle have the right to pledge or exchange those securitised assets without restriction.

Banks holding such securitised assets were also benefiting from lower capital charges. Under the standardised approach, securitised assets that received a credit rating from a rating agency were assigned the following risk weights: 20 percent for AAA to AA− ratings; 50 percent for A+ to A− ratings; and 100 percent for BBB+ to BBB− ratings. Banks that were authorised to use the IRB approach to determine the risk weights for securitised assets received a more generous reduction in capital requirements. This is best demonstrated in Box 3 that shows the applicable risk weights for different rating categories and seniority of claims on the asset pool. A securitisation exposure is treated as a senior tranche if it is effectively backed or secured by a first claim on the entire amount of the assets in the pool.

Box 3: Risk weights under IRB approach for securitised assets						
Claims seniority	AAA	AA	A+	A .	A−	BBB+
Senior	7%	8%	10%	12%	20%	35%
Other	12%	15%	18%	20%	35%	50%

Banks also received beneficial treatment on capital charges associated with how net exposures were to be calculated on collateralised financing transactions (that is, backed by some financial collateral and referred to as repo trades). These transactions are backed by legal documentation by which the banks will have the right to liquidate or take legal possession of the collateral in the event of default or bankruptcy of the counterparty. The revised Basel II standard allowed fuller offset of collateral against exposures by effectively reducing the exposure amount by the value of the collateral. This was made possible by allowing banks under the IRB approach to use their own estimates of haircuts on the collateral assets. Haircuts are amounts by which the value of an asset is reduced to be prudent in estimating the collateral value that can be recovered under liquidation in the event of counterparty default.

CHAPTER FIVE

SWISS CHOCOLATES

Whenever I travel outside Europe, I am now used to carrying a few boxes of Swiss chocolates with me. I know it is a highly regarded product that will find admirers anywhere in the world. Coming from Switzerland, my friends and relatives know that it is authentic even if they cannot tell the difference between a German, Belgian or Swiss chocolate from the taste. They simply trust me.

Luckily for the Swiss who are steeped in tradition, factories manufacturing chocolates in India, China or Africa have not managed to find a Chocolate Rating Agency that can provide the stamp "Swiss made" based on some set of quality control criteria. Suppose the Food and Drug Administration gives the authorisation to some agencies to do such branding. Then this business model would bring big money to the chocolate rating agencies if only they can charge a small fee for every box of chocolate that carries their stamp of authentication. It will be a win-win situation for all of us. I will benefit from paying lower prices for Swiss made chocolates to distribute to friends, everyone in the world will be able to buy Swiss chocolates at affordable prices, and chocolate factories around the world will be making huge profits.

Does it sound familiar? Well, replace Swiss chocolates by securitised assets rated AAA, Food and Drug Administration by Basel Committee, chocolate rating agencies by credit rating agencies, and chocolate factories by investment banks. The question in everyone's mind will be the following: "How did the chocolate factories around the world manage to produce Swiss chocolates, and what were the criteria to be met to get the Swiss made stamp on them?"

Let me provide the intuition behind an approach that the chocolate rating agencies might come up with in consultation with chocolate factories to establish the criteria for assigning the Swiss made stamp. Suppose the factories agree to produce 1.2 kilogram of assorted chocolates for every 1 kilogram of chocolates that will receive a Swiss made stamp. Consumers are then assured, as certified by the chocolate rating agencies, that at least 1 kilogram in a box containing 1.2 kilogram of chocolates is of Swiss quality. But they will have to pay only $20 compared to $30 to buy similar quality real Swiss chocolates which are very difficult to procure.

It is easy to see why this is a win-win situation for everyone. Consumers will be eager to buy them at discounted prices and they know that Swiss quality chocolates can be resold at a good price if they change their mind later. To give reassurances to consumers, the factories buy small quantities of Swiss rated chocolates from each other to demonstrate trust in the quality and pricing. For the chocolate factories this is a great business model because they are able to sell 1.2 kilogram of these chocolates without the Swiss quality stamp for only $15. Even after paying a commission of $1 to chocolate rating agencies that benefit from the evolving business strategy, chocolate factories are now making an addition profit of $4 on each box of chocolates sold. Moreover, with a health conscious younger generation, the consumption of chocolates is projected to decline and a new business strategy is needed to remain profitable. The Food and Drug Administration will be satisfied that Swiss chocolates, known for their high quality, do not pose any health hazard.

This in a nutshell was the asset securitisation business model that flourished, although there were other nuances as to how the assets were packaged and sold. Before I discuss some of the modelling assumptions that were used to create securitisation products, it is important to understand the changes that were taking place in financial markets since the late 1990s that required banks to come up with new business models to remain profitable. Let me elaborate on this.

One important change was the rapid growth of internet services leading to the emergence of more automated trading platforms and discount brokerage services. A second one was the introduction of the euro in 1999 that eliminated profits from transaction fees banks were used to making on foreign exchange trading in Europe. Both affected the commissions and fees banks could earn, which forced them to look for alternative sources of income.

Another important change, which I had mentioned earlier, was the flattening of the yield curve – that is interest rates becoming almost identical across various maturities. Banks that rely less on trading-related revenue have to generate profits from the interest spread they earn by borrowing short-term and lending long-term. When the interest spread between long-term and short term rates decline, so does the net interest income earned by banks.

Purchases of medium- and long-term bonds by central banks as their foreign currency reserves rose sharply in the period 2000 to 2005 was one factor contributing to yield curve flattening. But there were other factors too. The international accounting standards board (IASB), whose standards are followed in Europe, introduced a revised rule called IAS 19 in 1999. This required defined benefit pension liabilities to be discounted using the long-term yield on highly rated corporate bonds. As long-term yields fall, these liabilities rise, and this can translate to a deficit in pension assets to cover liabilities. Moreover, if pension assets are mainly invested in equities, and their market value falls in the same period when yields decline, then the pension fund deficit can increase further. Indeed, big fall in prices of equities during 2000 to 2002 while bond yields also fell at the same time highlighted these challenges.

The developments in this period led many pension funds to shift to an investment approach promoted by consultants called the "liability-driven strategy" which required a shift out of equities in favour of long-term bonds. At the same time, many life insurance companies also exposed to similar risks on their balance sheet started to embrace this strategy. The new technical standards for insurers in the EU called Solvency II, which was still in consultation phase, was promoting such practices. Because the level of interest income on the bonds they were buying had to be greater than the costs incurred on servicing the liabilities, it led to what was referred to at that time as a "search-for-yield". But investment restrictions on the credit quality of the bonds they were authorised to buy meant that this search-for-yield had to be met through highly rated bonds.

Investment banks were quick to spot the dilemma faced by institutional investors. They identified a growing demand for higher yields on top-notch rated bonds. Few corporates or governments could deliver on both requirements, and the supply of US Treasury bonds at that time was declining or only increasing modestly. All that investment banks had to do was to come up with innovative solutions to create securities that met both requirements of institutional investors. They also recognised that smaller regional and retail banks themselves could be interested in such products under the Basel II regime. For this game plan, large universal and investment banks needed the support of credit rating agencies.

As banks and credit rating agencies got down to their drawing boards to decide how to structure these products with financial engineers, they managed to influence the Basel II rules on treatment of securitised products and off-balance sheet exposures in ways that would benefit banks' new business model. This new business model came to be known as the "originate and distribute" model. Due to a lack of historical data on the newly securitised assets, Basel Committee's decisions on capital treatment of these assets were guided by results of stress tests presented by banks and credit rating agencies. At the same time, the capital treatment rules on credit commitments given to off-balance sheet vehicles in which these assets were parked before distribution provided plenty of room for manoeuvre. Both turned out to be costly mistakes made by the Basel Committee.

But what are securitised assets or securitisations? And how do they differ from other debt securities that pay regular coupons or interest income and principal at maturity? The Basel Committee under the Basel II standard defines a traditional securitisation as a structure where the cash flows from an underlying pool of exposures are used to service at least two tranches that reflect different degrees of credit risk. Payment of the debt obligations to the investors should depend on the performance of the specified underlying exposures, as opposed to being derived from an obligation of the entity originating those exposures.

Let me try to explain what this means focusing on the first question in the above paragraph. Most of us are familiar with the use of credit cards to purchase goods. Each purchase is a loan extended by the bank issuing the credit card. The monthly interest and amortisation payments we make become receivables to the bank. The bank issuing the credit card can sell these receivables from many credit card customers to a special purpose vehicle (SPV). Usually, the legal form used for credit cards is a trust structure, but this a technical issue. In practice, the receivables being transferred can come from auto loans, student loans or even trade receivables.

The receivables transferred to the SPV are then packaged into two classes of securities, one which is a senior tranche and another which is a junior tranche. The senior tranche is sold to investors and the proceeds are paid to the bank. But the transferring bank retains its exposures to the junior tranche, which only pays out if all the claims of the senior tranche have been met. This securitisation structure has existed for many years dating back to the 1980s, and it goes under the name of asset-backed securities (ABS). These securities are usually rated by credit rating agencies to facilitate sales to institutional investors.

Concerning the second question, there are essentially two key differences between debt securities issued by, say a corporate or a bank, and a securitisation product. First, the cash flows based on which the interest and principal payments on the securitisation product are paid to investors are restricted to the receivables in the SPV. Second, the junior tranche of the securitisation product can absorb losses without interrupting the contractual payments to the investors in the senior tranche. In a standard debt security, losses can be transferred to a subordinate debt holder only when the entity issuing debt is put to liquidation.

These traditional forms of securitisations mentioned here did not play much of a role in triggering or feeding into the financial crisis. These securitisation products were well understood by investors, and credit rating agencies had sufficient historical data to make assessments about their credit quality. Moreover, the receivables being securitised were those originated by large bank holding companies in the United States that were in this business for many years. By retaining their exposures to the junior tranche, these banks were subject to capital charges on them. At the same time, retention of exposures in a junior tranche forced banks to be prudent in screening borrowers.

The main innovation in securitisation markets that turned out to be toxic was the structuring of certain categories of residential mortgage loans. The originators of these loans were both specialised mortgage lenders as well as large depository banks. Lehman Brothers, Bear Stearns, Merrill Lynch and Countrywide Securities were leading underwriters of these mortgage loans, meaning they acquired these loans on their books. The business model of the mortgage originators and underwriters was built on exploiting the weakness in some elements of Basel II rules that included the risk weights applicable for securitisation products, ability to recognise full risk transfer benefits when these loans were sold, and benefiting from exceedingly low capital charges on credit commitments to entities sponsored by banks.

What was the technology used to package inedible chocolates and sell them as Swiss quality chocolates? Putting this into context, what modelling assumptions were used by credit rating agencies to take a bundle of junk-rated bonds or low quality loans and label a part of that bundle as being similar in quality to US Treasuries? Being of similar quality to US Treasuries simply means that the probability of not receiving the interest and principal due on the security is very low for investors.

Let me focus on bonds issued by a collection of junk-rated firms to illustrate the underlying principle. Suppose there are 1,000 of these firms each of which has issued $1 million worth of junk-rated bonds paying an annual coupon or interest rate of 10 percent. Let us assume that these firms do diverse business and are in different geographical regions. The earnings of these firms, which are used to repay the debt, will be affected by global and local macroeconomic developments apart from company-specific risks. It is reasonable to assume that the earnings risk faced by each firm will be exposed to some common factors, but the overall risks are substantially reduced through diversification by holding a portfolio of these junk bonds. This is exactly the same principle that works when we invest in a diversified stock market index rather than a single stock to reduce the risk of large losses.

Turning to the portfolio of junk bonds that are assumed to mature in one year, let us think of setting up a SPV that will buy these bonds of 1,000 firms. To do this, the SPV needs $1 billion funding. An investment or universal bank can step in to provide temporary credit for the assurance that it will have the right to sell securities to be issued by the SPV backed by these bonds to investors. A credit rating agency examines the average historical annual default rate of such firms and concludes that this is 4 percent per annum, and about 50 cents on a dollar cannot be recovered upon default. This calculation will show that about $20 million from the non-performing assets can be recovered.

Now the SPV with bonds worth $1 billion on the asset side of its balance sheet paying 10 percent interest rate will issue at least two classes of securities backed by the junk bonds to investors. As an example, one will be senior bonds rated AAA worth $600 million and paying 5 percent interest rate per annum. The other will be $300 million worth of junior bonds rated BBB and paying 8 percent interest rate. The remaining $100 million will be sold to equity investors who have a residual claim on the SPV assets. The bond ratings will be validated by a credit rating agency for which they receive $2 million fees. An additional amount of $4 million will be set aside for operating costs of the company.

It is simple to work out the math in this case and figure out the expected payoff for the equity investor. After taking recovery on defaulted bonds into account, the SPV assets will amount to $1,076 million after interest and principal payments from non-defaulted firms are received. On the liability side, the amount due to bond investors plus the expenses incurred will be equal to $960 million. The difference equal to $116 million on the liability side that balances the accounts of the SPV will be the share belonging to equity investors. Having invested only $100 million, the annual rate of return to the equity holders in this example will be 16 percent.

The example I discussed above gives the intuition behind the financial engineering that helps create securitisation products with different claims priority. The legal structure is such that the SPV does not have to be dissolved to force losses on the junior bond holders if equity claims are wiped out. A rating agency will report that the overcollateralisation level for the senior bond holder in this structure is 166 percent computed as the ratio of size of total assets divided by the size of total liabilities of the senior tranche.

In arriving at the ratings of the two classes of bonds issued, a portfolio credit risk model will be employed by the credit rating agency which is then subject to a number of stressed risk scenarios. One would be an increase in the likelihood of joint defaults; another would be an increase in the probability of individual defaults; and perhaps a third one will be lower recovery values on the debt when a firm defaults.

How would the simple calculations I illustrated above stand up to such stressed scenarios? Those who closely followed my number crunching would have immediately recognised that I was using the expected loss formula I introduced in the earlier chapter to estimate the upfront write-off to be $20 million for equity investors. This was calculated by taking the product of exposure at default of $1 billion, the probability of default of 4 percent, and the loss given default of 50 percent. But I also introduced in that chapter the term unexpected loss which will require capital allocation under the Basel II rules. The credit rating agencies will be computing the capital cushion needed under some risk scenarios to determine the ratings of the senior and junior bonds in our example.

Let us try to compute this capital requirement making the assumption that the asset side of the SPV comprises mortgage loans instead of junk bonds. This will help us understand the limitations of models when I subsequently try to highlight how cracks appeared when subprime mortgage loans were packaged and securitised. The Basel II rules for capital requirement K in Box 2 in Chapter 4 will have to be multiplied by the exposure at default (EAD) of $1 billion to arrive at the amount of capital needed at a 99.9 percent confidence level. I will use the correlation value R=0.15, probability of default PD=0.04, and loss given default LGD=0.5 for the base case scenario. Calculations will show that the capital needed is $46 million to withstand unexpected losses under Basel II rules. If this loss is factored in, equity investors will make a 30 percent loss on their investment. The probability that losses could exceed this amount will be one in a thousand since we computed the loss amount at a 99.9 percent confidence level. Under the base case risk scenario, the junior bond holders will receive all their principal and interest payments promised.

The credit rating agency may impose an adverse risk scenario under which the loss parameters increase substantially in order to assess if their AAA tranche rating can still be supported. Suppose such a stress scenario requires the following choices: PD=0.08; LGD=0.75; and R=0.25. Capital requirement calculations will show that besides setting aside expected loss amount of $60 million under the new parameters, the SPV will need an additional $220 million to cover unexpected losses at 99.9 percent confidence level. In this scenario, equity investors will we wiped out, but junior bond holders will still recover 60 percent of their investment. Senior bond holders will receive promised interest and principal payments without having to take any losses.

The models and assumptions being used by credit rating agencies had been developed by academics, and broadly the same modelling ideas were used in Basel II rules for computing credit risk capital requirements. The banking supervisors were happy to let markets regulate themselves as long as they operated within the framework agreed upon to monitor, manage and mitigate credit risk. The fresh graduates in physics, mathematics and engineering hired by credit rating agencies to do the number crunching exercise were delighted to have a well-paid job. Trust that the innovations in finance will deliver new levels of economic prosperity reached a peak. There were some sceptics though, including the Bank for International Settlements.

With the technology established for creating highly rated debt securities that provide yield enhancements over traditional bonds of similar ratings, banks needed to complete a third and final leg to set in motion their new business model. This required identifying borrowers with low credit quality. Basel II rules provided banks adequate escape routes to ensure that their balance sheet will only be exposed to trading book capital charges for a brief period during the origination and securitisation phase before distribution.

The loan volumes to be generated and the interest spread over US Treasuries required on them to offer attractive yields on securitisation assets to institutional investors meant that the US residential mortgage market had to be targeted. Borrowers with good credit standing and seeking mortgage loans below some threshold amount were already having access to credit through government-sponsored mortgage agencies like Fannie Mae and Freddie Mac.

Several banks and originators of mortgage loans focused on borrowers with lower credit scores so that the loans they extended qualified as subprime mortgage loans justifying higher interest rates to be charged. There were different tweaks and tricks offered to borrowers to convince them how their mortgage payments will be serviceable in an environment of generally rising house prices. The total volume of non-agency mortgage loans that were underwritten amounted to $4.3 trillion in the period 2004–2006. The volume of subprime mortgage loans originated amounted to $1.75 trillion in this period. Nearly 75 percent of subprime mortgage loans originated were securitised and sold to investors.

But let me return to the modelling framework that was used to assign credit ratings to different tranches of the securities issued by the SPV. Why did the risk model go so wrong for securitisation products backed by subprime mortgage loans? This is in stark contrast to risk models for securitisation of prime mortgage loans, auto loans and credit card loans that had performed quite well for decades. A simple answer to the question is that the validity of a model's prediction relies on the appropriateness of the assumptions used to derive the model parameters.

Let us take the example of a model used to predict the distance required to bring a car to a halt when it is travelling at a speed of 50 kilometres per hour. The model used to estimate this will require as inputs the quality of the tyres and the conditions of the road to calculate the frictional forces that come into play in addition to the weight of the car. The model might predict that the car will come to a halt in 5 metres. If the car is travelling on a road covered with a thin layer of ice, the model's prediction will be completely wrong. In this case we will have to recalculate the frictional forces when there is ice on the road and update the model parameters to get a correct prediction of the distance travelled before the car comes to a halt.

The model parameters used to assign credit ratings for securitised assets backed by subprime mortgage loans were calibrated to good weather conditions, speed limits applicable for city driving and common standards for the quality of tyres used in cars. But the car drivers were reckless because the cars they were driving did not belong to them – meaning they did not have to pay for damages if there was an accident. This is the philosophy behind the originate-and-distribute business model. The policemen on the road were absent, that is the regulators were confident that sophisticated market participants will follow rules and punish erring members through market discipline. The drivers pretended not to know there was a layer of ice on the road that would make stopping difficult – that is banks packaging the subprime loans ignored the fact that the screening of borrower's credit quality was poor.

The credit rating agencies also did not do their homework. Or, perhaps they knew but were worried that if they would recognise it and alter the parameters of the credit risk model, it would result in different tranche ratings – probably closer to junk quality – and destroy an important revenue stream from rating securitisation products. Indeed, if we set PD=0.08, LGD=0.5 and R=0.6, both the equity as well as the junior bondholders' claims will be wiped out and the senior bond holders may recover only 90 percent of their investments. The default rate of subprime borrowers taking adjustable rate mortgages reached a peak of over 40 percent in 2009.

I would like to draw attention here to the fact that when we raise the correlation parameter R in the credit risk model from 0.15 recommended in Basel II to 0.6, pooling of subprime mortgage loans would never support a triple-A rated tranche to be issued. Returning to the example of the braking distance for a car, when frictional forces are high, a few cars crashing could be attributed to rash or poor driving skills of the drivers. The others can stop in time to avoid accidents justifying a low value for R. But if the road has a layer of ice, all you need is a few cars to crash and the rest that follow behind cannot stop in time under these conditions to avoid accidents. In the case of borrowers of subprime mortgage loans, good weather conditions meant rising house prices that will justify the use of R=0.15. But when house prices fall, this is equivalent to having ice on the road. It will require significant increase in correlation of joint defaults in the credit risk model to make right predictions. The inexperienced fresh graduates that did the mathematical modelling for credit rating agencies for rating securitised products had never been through winters.

This reminds me of the famous quote of Einstein who said that god does not play dice with the universe. This is the case when we deal with engineering systems whose dynamical behaviour can be described by the laws of physics that allow us to derive a model and its parameters using objective reasoning. But bankers do play dice with the financial markets. Consequently, there is significant amount of behavioural elements that underpin how financial markets function, and this requires the model and its parameters describing the evolution of financial variables to be derived based on subjective reasoning. That is prone to error.

But why do mortgage loans in America have propensity to default in large numbers when house prices fall compared to what is observed in other countries? The reason for this is that the US mortgage loan market has a feature not shared widely across other jurisdictions. This feature is the limited liability of the homeowner taking a mortgage loan, who has the right to drop the keys of the house or the apartment to the bank and walk away if he decides not to pay interest on the loan. The technical term used is that they are non-recourse loans. Such loans allow a lender to only foreclose and take possession of the collateral, but cannot take further legal action if the sale proceeds do not recover the outstanding loan amount.

While there are some advantages to granting non-recourse loans, such as ease of foreclosure and forcing banks to recognise non-performing mortgage loans early, it does make the US financial system procyclical, a criticism that was also made against Basel II standards. Mitigating this would require establishing regulatory caps on loan-to-value ratios for housing loans and enforcing stricter standards for credit screening of borrowers. But this may interfere with the American dream of home ownership.

In defence of the Basel Committee responsible for setting global standards for capital requirements and regulation, the US mortgage lending practice was an outlier. But the lessons learned through identification of the channels for regulatory arbitrage helped tighten regulatory standards not only in supervision but also in other areas. And it helped US Congress approve legislation for a fundamental overhaul of the US financial system with Wall Street lobbying power being blunted after the crisis.

The pooling of loans and securitising them to distribute various tranches with different credit ratings to a variety of investors did not stop just with subprime mortgage loans. The period 2004 to 2007 also saw large increase in the issuance volumes of syndicated loans by banks to fund leveraged buyouts and merger and acquisition activities. Such financing goes under the name leveraged loans which refer to corporate debt with relatively high credit risk. Market participants refer to this loan origination process as syndication rather than underwriting – a term that is used for bonds.

Until the late 1990s, leveraged loans were usually syndicated to groups of banks at origination and held to maturity by the syndicate members with little secondary market trading. But the landscape of leveraged loans changed significantly around 2002 as issuance volumes started growing rapidly with institutional investors replacing banks as main investors. This was accompanied by borrower-friendly terms of loan issuance, including weaker covenant protection terms for lenders. The main buyers of these leveraged loans from banks were securitisation vehicles, which went under the name collateralised loan obligation (CLO) vehicles, or simply as cash CLOs. Close to half of the leveraged loan demand came from these securitisation vehicles. Between 2004 and 2007 these securitisation vehicles bought nearly $700 billion of leverage loans.

The business model of these vehicles was the same as those of SPVs that bought subprime mortgage loans. The leveraged loans were securitised, and tranches of different ratings were issued under the name of CLOs. The different CLO notes sold to asset managers, other institutional investors and banks had little aggregate maturity mismatch to the underlying loans that backed them. This helped reduce risks that certain other structuring mechanisms faced.

The growth of CLO vehicles also fed into banks' new strategy of developing the originate-and-distribute business model. Banks' profits were now derived from the fees they were generating from different activities surrounding the leveraged loan market: fees received for arranging the loans; fees and trading profits associated with market-making in the secondary markets; and fees and underwriting revenues associated with assisting CLO managers to set up and fund their vehicles.

What I have described so far laid the foundations for banks to intermediate rapid credit growth that was out of sync with the pace of economic activity. By not being exposed to the risks that these loans may default one day, banks felt that it was someone else's problem to do due diligence and risk assessment of the new financial instruments; and the credit rating agencies were providing valuable help. Yet, while these securitisation products played an instrumental role in amplifying the crisis, they were not the triggers for the financial crisis. Mechanisms that had the power to trigger the crisis were being set up through resecuritisation of these securitised products. As the name suggests, these schemes issued liabilities whose repayments were backed by some or all of the cash flows generated by securitised assets.

I will try to focus on two specific resecuritisation schemes that bought securitised assets and issued liabilities backed by these assets to investors. These were the asset-backed commercial paper (ABCP) conduits and structured investment vehicles (SIVs). Each of them had different business models as regards how they were set up and managed, but both shared one common feature. This was in buying securitised and other assets whose average maturity was greater than the average maturity of the liabilities issued to investors to fund these assets. This construct turned out to be the spark that ignited the financial fire in the second half of 2007. Let me explain below the main features of these two resecuritisation vehicles.

Banks have always funded some of their assets by issuing short-term certificates of deposit whose average maturity is typically around 30 days. These instruments are not collateralised, meaning the investors are paid from the general cash flows generated by the bank issuing them. With the shift towards originate-and-distribute business model starting around 2000, banks were constantly exploring ways to avoid incurring capital charges on the assets they had underwritten. The ABCP conduits which had existed for many years provided banks with yet another vehicle for regulatory capital arbitrage under the new Basel standards. Set up as a SPV, these conduits were used to buying trade receivables and then issuing commercial paper backed by these assets. This helped non-financial corporations to raise cash to meet their liquidity needs by selling trade receivables to the conduits. Because investors' claims were backed by the assets in a bankruptcy remote vehicle, the short-term liabilities issued by them received the name asset-backed commercial paper or simple ABCP.

With their new business model in place, banks began setting up ABCP conduits which they sponsored. That is, they supplied them with the assets that they did not want to hold on their balance sheet, and then extended liquidity support to the conduits through credit commitments. The liquidity support was required because the cash flows from assets held by the conduits did not always match the cash outflows needed to pay the liability claims. The conduits also had material maturity mismatches between the assets they held and liabilities they issued. Typical assets held included securitisation assets, trade receivables and other consumer loans. To provide some tangible figures, I have extracted below the disclosure made by Deutsche Bank in its 2007 Annual Report.

"We originate and administer our own asset-backed commercial paper (ABCP) programs. Some conduits remain off-balance sheet because we are not deemed to control them; these have assets totalling € 4.8 billion which consist of securities backed by non-US residential mortgages issued by warehouse SPVs set up by the sellers to facilitate the purchase of the assets by the conduits. The minimum credit rating for these securities is AA-. The credit enhancement necessary to achieve the required credit ratings is ordinarily provided by mortgage insurance extended by third-party insurers to the SPVs. The weighted-average life of the assets held in the conduits is 5 years. The average life of the commercial paper issued by these off-balance sheet conduits is one to three months. Our exposure to these entities is limited to the committed liquidity facilities entered into by us to provide funding to the conduits in the event of market disruption. The committed liquidity facilities to these conduits total € 6.3 billion and we are the only liquidity facility provider to these entities."

The maturity mismatch built into the bank-sponsored conduits was necessary to generate excess spread between the interest earned on the assets and the interest paid on the liabilities. This net interest margin earned was used to pay various costs incurred by the ABCP conduits. These were: operating costs; fees to the bank providing the liquidity support; and insurance costs to obtain external credit enhancement to cover potential credit losses on the assets held. I would like to mention here that when the value of assets exceeded liabilities resulting in overcollateralisation to benefit liability holders (Swiss chocolate example), the support was called internal credit enhancement.

Credit rating agencies rated these conduits on the basis of the strength of liquidity support and credit enhancement arrangements. It was important for sponsoring banks to ensure that the ABCP conduits received AA− rating or better. By structuring the liquidity support or the credit commitments to be less than one year, banks reporting under the advanced internal ratings-based approach could choose the appropriate credit conversion factor (CCF) for the support. By setting CCF as 20 percent, which was the requirement for banks reporting under the standardised approach of Basel II, the risk weights for these credit commitments would be only 4 percent of the total exposure. Sponsoring banks earned fees both from the liquidity support provided as well as from the market-making activities to sell the liabilities of the conduits.

The other resecuritisation scheme employed was the structured investment vehicle. The assets held by the SIVs were very similar to those of the ABCP conduits, that is, they also invested in securitised assets with an average maturity of 3 to 4 years. But SIVs tended to manage their assets actively to meet some of their liquidity needs. This required that they held more liquid assets compared to the ABCP conduits. SIVs' business model also differed from those of conduits in the sense that they issued multiple liabilities with different seniority of claims. These included senior debt, subordinated capital notes and some equity. Senior debt usually constituted short-term paper, which were also sold under the name ABCP for being backed by the SIVs' assets, and medium-term notes. Capital notes were junior claims. Together with equity, they constituted about 7 to 10 percent of the liabilities of SIVs.

As the average liabilities were 1 to 2 years lower than that of the assets held, SIVs required some liquidity support from banks beyond what they could generate from active trading. But this liquidity support seldom covered 100 percent of their issuance unlike the case for ABCP conduits. By mid-2007, out of 34 SIVs that were operating and managing $400 billion worth of assets, 19 SIVs were sponsored by banks and controlled about 85 percent of the market share.

It was a no brainer for market participants and regulators to recognise that these resecuritisation vehicles were following a business model very similar to that of traditional banks. That is, the business model involved lending long-term (buying long-term assets) and borrowing short-term (issuing short-term liabilities). This meant there was a maturity transformation, and because the long-term assets were less liquid than the short-term claims they sold, there was also a liquidity transformation.

Providing liquidity and maturity transformations to the economy, which is done by collecting redeemable deposits from individuals and then making long term loans to firms and entrepreneurs, is the core business of banking. To safeguard against the risks of a run on bank deposits, there is a compulsory bank deposit insurance scheme to which banks pay an insurance premium. Beyond this, central banks provide liquidity backstop arrangements to banks and regulate their activities by requiring them to hold capital commensurate with the risks they take.

For the resecuritisation vehicles discussed above, banks acted as their central bank by providing liquidity support. Credit rating agencies acted as their regulators by reviewing their risk management practices and backstop arrangements, and then granting them AA or AAA ratings after collecting a fee. But entities like ABCP conduits and SIVs did not have to comply with any capital requirement standards, and yet were copying the banking business model. Consequently, they came to be called "shadow banks".

So far, I have emphasised the operational features and the different forms of support needed to obtain high credit ratings for the conduits and SIVs. Among them, the external credit enhancement secured by these vehicles is an important feature that is examined by rating agencies. This is because there is always some risk that debtors whose assets are held by the resecuritisation vehicle may fail to repay their debt. The ABCP conduits in particular, may have little or no equity cushion to absorb these losses depending on whether it has some or no overcollateralisation.

To remedy this, ABCP conduits and SIVs often needed an external credit enhancement to satisfy rating agencies. But a resecuritisation vehicle that wants to be rated AA or better must secure the credit enhancement from a firm that has the same or a better rating. That constraint did not leave many firms to choose from, and the only firms that had such high credit ratings were insurance companies. Monoline insurance companies, which were in the business of insuring US municipal bonds, were pleased to step in. Generally, this credit enhancement was provided in the form of a guarantee, also called monoline wraps, and it required quarterly premiums to be paid to monoline insurers commensurate with the credit risk being insured.

Larger insurance firms, including the American International Group (AIG), also provided such credit guarantees. Instead of guaranteeing the resecuritisation vehicles, it was also common to insure the securitised assets themselves to improve their rating. As the originate-and-distribute business model flourished, monoline insurers started riding this wave to generate additional fee income by providing securitisation assets and resecuritisation vehicles with credit guarantees using their status as AAA rated firms.

Every actor's involvement improved the trust in the financial system. In this environment, no investor managing serious amounts of money wanted to display their ignorance in front of expensively clad bank sales teams as they preached the virtues of three and four letter word products that offered mouth-watering yield pick-ups over conventional instruments. But the investors did not realise that these sales people were not as smart as the vegetable vendors on the streets of Chennai who understood every detail of the products they were selling.

All this created significant interlinkages among financial players in such a way that if one link that supported this new financial architecture were to break, the whole structure would collapse. It wasn't that this architecture took many years to build so that regulators had time to analyse and respond. The unprecedented growth in these financial products happened just in a matter of two years from 2005 to 2006 while central banks were still grappling with the new terminologies before trying to assess the risks they posed. To provide some numbers on this rapid growth in structured finance, the outstanding amounts of short-term ABCP debt increased from $680 billion in December 2001 to only $690 billion in December 2004, but then jumped to $1.1 trillion in December 2006. It all happened very fast.

CHAPTER SIX

MULTIPLE LINKS

Over the years I have come to realise how hard it is to make sense of the acronyms and trader jargon if you do not work in the financial industry. So far, I have tried to introduce some of this jargon in ways that would be accessible to many on the main street. They are important building blocks for understanding the structures that were used to build financial castles. But I need to introduce many more instruments, players and terminology before I can provide deeper insights into the forces that fuelled the financial crisis. These additional instruments can be thought of as the glue that held the different building blocks of the financial castle together. Every block of the castle was connected to one another using this glue, and if ruptures were to occur in these important joints, the whole castle was designed to crash. Were bankers and Wall Street worried? They were not paid to worry, and anyway it was someone else's job. Were regulators aware of this? I will defer the answer to the next chapter.

I have been describing so far the developments that were taking place in the United States in the run-up to the financial crisis. One can say that the multiple links among financial market participants that these practices created were driven by supply side developments in structured finance. But demand side developments for these products created interlinkages with banks in Europe as well as with US money market mutual funds. At the same time, interconnections among banks within Europe started growing rapidly following the introduction of the euro. Interdependencies between banks and financial market participants are generally not a cause for concern. Such dependencies are essential for developing deeper and efficient capital markets. But there were certain market practices that made these links fragile. They were in some sense time bombs that were just waiting for a trigger to explode.

Before digging deeper into these market practices that were brewing trouble, let me provide some background on what was happening in the European banking industry some years before the crisis. Focusing more narrowly on banks in the euro area, the common currency as well as the common monetary policy framework created a huge demand for housing finance as borrowing rates fell in the peripheral countries. In normal circumstances, the banking system of a country will finance this loan demand largely through the deposits they have collected, and excess loan demand will be met by issuance of bank debt. Interest rates on bank debt are usually higher than rates paid on bank deposits. If more loans are to be met through issuance of bank debt, the interest rates on bank loans will rise as banks pass the higher interest costs to borrowers. Further, the central bank of the country is likely to take actions to dampen loan growth if it is perceived to be excessive by employing a variety of tools, including by raising short-term interest rates.

These standard mechanisms to moderate loan growth were taken out of the tool kit by adopting a common monetary policy applicable to the entire euro area. On the flip side, the adoption of a common currency aided Germany's export sector in generating a large current account surplus by mitigating currency appreciation pressures. This period also saw rising German household savings while domestic loan demand remained weak, and these together led to excess funds in German banks that required investment outlets. Lack of investment opportunities eroded profits and state-owned German banks (Landesbanken) were most hard hit. As this period coincided with rising profits across the broader banking industry driven by the originate-and-distribute business model, finding alternative investment solutions to improve profitability became pressing for the smaller German banks.

Against this background, the smaller German banks pursued a two pronged strategy. One was to lend their excess funds through the interbank market to banks in the peripheral euro area countries, and this strategy tended to favour Spanish and Irish banks. The other strategy was to buy highly rated securitised products backed by subprime mortgage and other assets originated in the United States to boost profits by holding these higher yielding securities.

The first strategy of providing peripheral euro area countries access to large interbank funding introduced new linkages among euro area banks. German banks were not alone in following this strategy. French banks also had significant exposure to banks in the peripheral euro countries through the interbank market. British banks, on the other hand, were more linked to Irish banks and were funding a large share of the excess demand for housing finance. The interbank lending, which has typical maturities of one week to one month, is uncollateralised and is one of the least resilient source of funding for banks. This is because banks cut this lending first to a bank that is perceived to have problems.

The second strategy of buying securitised assets was pursued not only by German banks but also by other European banks, including the large Swiss banks. As regards this strategy, the question in everyone's mind will be: "But what incentivised German and other European banks to buy securitised assets originated in the United States?" A less reported, less understood and perhaps deliberately underplayed reason for this is that the US never managed to get its act together to implement Basel II, whereas Europe did this already in 2005. This had profound implications for banks in Europe which found it attractive to buy highly rated securitised assets due to the lower risk weights attached to them under Basel II.

This is to be contrasted with developments in the United States where regulators announced that they want only the large international banks to comply with the advanced internal ratings-based approach and let smaller banks report their capital adequacy ratios following the Basel I standard. As a result, the US banks did not find it attractive to buy securitised products due to the higher capital charges on them. Subprime loans were mainly bought by US mortgage agencies that had an explicit mandate to promote home ownership in the United States.

European banks, however, could not simply buy securitised assets denominated in US dollars because they did not have their liabilities funded in dollars. In the smaller regional banks, liabilities were mainly in the form of retail deposits collected in the local currency, which was the euro for many European banks. To mitigate or hedge the currency risks involved when buying dollar-denominated assets, banks had to execute additional trades. This would involve selling euros to buy US dollars in a spot transaction, and then the proceeds will be used to buy the dollar-denominated securitised assets. At the same time, the bank would hedge the currency risk by executing another trade through a universal bank. This trade would involve a forward sale of US dollars in exchange for euros at some future date, typically in one or three months' time. This would eliminate the currency risk incurred as a result of purchasing US securitised assets.

The transactions mentioned above can be executed under one trade called the foreign exchange (FX) swap or simply the FX swap. As an example of a one-month FX swap transaction, a German regional bank would sell euros at the current spot exchange rate to receive US dollars from a universal bank such as Deutsche Bank. The FX swap contract would entitle the regional bank to receive euros in one month time in exchange for US dollars at a rate called the forward FX rate. If the one month interbank interest rates for the euro and the US dollar happen to be identical, the spot and forward FX rates will be the same. The exchange of currencies at the beginning and at the end of the deal ensures that the transaction is collateralised so that there is no counterparty risk.

The notion that counterparty risk is mitigated is true only in theory. Banks recognise that if the counterpart to the transaction defaults, typically through bankruptcy, then the non-defaulted counterpart or bank will be left with a currency that it does not need. Again, taking the example of the German regional bank, its default will result in Deutsche Bank being left with euros even though it was expecting to receive US dollars at the time the transaction would close out.

The fact is that despite having the notion that the FX swap is a collateralised transaction, banks do not necessarily view it that way. In the event of failure of the regional German bank, Deutsche Bank will have to sell euros in the FX spot market to raise US dollars. This FX rate can be quite different from the forward rate agreed at the time the FX swap transaction was entered.

Recognising this risk, the risk management division of Deutsche Bank will withdraw authorisation to do further deals with the regional bank if its credit risk rises significantly. If the regional bank now holds the US securitised asset and cannot raise dollars by selling euros, what is typically done by rolling over the FX swap trade, it will be forced to liquidate the securitised asset if it wants to eliminate currency risk on its balance sheet.

The question one would want to raise here is the following. "Under what circumstances will Deutsche Bank decide not to roll-over the FX swap transaction?"

I noted earlier that the heightened risk of default of the counterparty is one reason. But there are number of other factors that also come into play. They are linked to how Deutsche Bank goes about raising US dollars in the market after receiving euros from the regional bank, and the resilience of those funding sources. I will emphasise here two approaches that were predominantly used to raise dollar funds. One is by entering into an identical FX swap as the regional bank did, but this time with a US bank counterpart. This trade would pass the euros to the US bank and Deutsche Bank would receive US dollars against this, which then will be passed to the regional bank so that it can buy a US dollar-denominated securitised asset.

Another alternative for Deutsche Bank would be to issue certificates of deposit (CD) to raise dollar funds and pass this to the regional bank. If this approach is taken, the euros received from the regional bank would be used to buy short-term bonds or bills of any euro area government that carries zero risk weight in order to avoid incurring capital charges. The buyers of the CD would normally be US money market mutual funds or collective investment vehicles domiciled in Dublin or Luxembourg that offer US dollar investment funds to investors.

What I would like to draw attention to here is the multiple links among different financial players created by pursuing a simple strategy of a buying a US securitised asset by a European bank. In normal market conditions, these links should not be a cause for concern. In fact, it is tempting to argue that by bringing in different players into the financial market place, the risk-bearing capacity of the system as a whole should be strengthened. But in real life it does not work that way. If you hear an announcement in the football stadium that there is a mad man with one bullet in his gun and looking for a target, your chances of survival are higher if the stadium hosts 50,000 rather than 5,000 people. But how many really want to stay in the stadium and watch the game irrespective of the number of spectators in the stadium? In a similar vein, if you hear the rumour that one large bank might default, not much lending will take place to any bank if the system as a whole is interconnected.

Returning to the question when Deutsche Bank will not roll-over the FX swap with the regional bank, this will happen when Deutsche Bank itself faces constraints in raising dollar funds from the market or from a US bank. If the US bank has less need for euros, then it may put limits on the volume of FX swap transactions being done when counterparty risks rise. Also, when the US banks' own needs for dollar funding rises, it will not provide dollars to European banks. This happened when some conduits or SIVs sponsored by US banks had to be taken on their balance sheet when they faced funding problems.

Perhaps one detail that was overlooked or not effectively monitored by the central banking community in the run up to the crisis is the extent of excess demand for US dollars among European banks over a corresponding demand for euros among US banks. As European banks cannot borrow US dollars from their respective central banks, any disruption to dollar funding through financial markets would spell disaster. Not paying adequate attention early on to European banks dollar funding needs turned out to be a costly mistake.

Let me provide some indicative numbers on the size of the dollar funding needs faced by European banks based on the BIS banking statistics to put things in perspective. US dollar denominated assets held by European banks (euro area, Swiss and UK banks) rose from $5 trillion in September 2004 to $8.8 trillion in September 2007. By contrast, assets in European currencies (euros, Swiss francs, and pound sterling) held by US banks were only $0.5 trillion in September 2004 and rose to $0.8 trillion in September 2007.

The large US dollar funding needs of European banks had to be met through different means that included: funding by issuing certificates of deposits sold to US money market mutual funds; issuance of dollar-denominated bank bonds; attracting US dollar deposit placements from central bank reserve managers and from the BIS that intermediated these placements; and raising dollar funds through repo operations with US banks or money market mutual funds. Unfunded positions had to be hedged using FX swaps or derivative trades. Many of these funding options were simply not available to small regional banks. Consequently, they had to rely on large universal banks to meet their dollar funding needs. By establishing branches or subsidiaries in the United States, large universal banks had access to deposit funding, but as these banks focused less on retail business, the deposit collection base remained small.

Another way of looking at the aggregate excess US dollar exposure of European banks is to examine the difference between the dollar-denominated assets and the dollar-denominated liabilities banks held. If this difference is positive, it would imply that there is a net US dollar exposure to be hedged, and it is done typically by entering into a FX swap transaction. In mid-2007 this net US dollar exposure amounted to $800 billion, a size large enough to disrupt financial markets if a sudden spike in counterparty risk concerns put even a temporary halt to trading of FX swaps.

The funding instruments mentioned above to raise US dollars were mostly short term instruments excluding bank bonds with typical maturities being one week to one month. This made them susceptible to sudden disruptions when there is bad news, and the volumes involved were too large to quickly seek alternative sources. There were simply no alternative sources of dollar funding available. With so many interconnected players involved in meeting European banks' dollar funding needs, no link or funding source in this network could be put even temporarily out of service. These links proved to be disastrous and transformed the subprime crisis into a global crisis.

This is a good time to transition to another demand side development for securitised assets that played a dominant role in fuelling the financial crisis. No analysis of the financial crisis is complete without a discussion of the role US money market mutual funds played as a consequence of their collective actions. The so-called prime US money market mutual funds that invest in non-government short-term instruments had assets under management exceeding $1.5 trillion in end-2006. At that time, prime funds were holding about 60 percent of their assets in ABCP and other commercial paper issued by corporates. By end-2007 they were not buying ABCP as the conduits issuing them came under scrutiny.

The main reason for this change in investment behaviour is that the US Securities and Exchange Commission (SEC) regulates the credit quality of instruments that money market mutual funds are allowed to buy. This is based on ratings of these instruments published by credit rating agencies. In 2005 and 2006, the high quality ratings and better returns on ABCP instruments made them an attractive asset to hold for money market funds. But when the ratings of the conduits issuing them were downgraded subsequently, money market funds simply could not hold these instruments under the US SEC rules. By hard wiring credit ratings into regulation similar to the Basel II standards, the aggregate behaviour of money market funds, which were simply reacting to comply with regulatory requirements, caused severe disruptions to short term funding markets.

Money market funds were also important providers of liquidity to banks through repo financing. Many of the securitised assets that banks held before distribution were funded in repo markets. This involves lending the securitised asset as collateral to a counterpart, often times a money market mutual fund, and receive cash in exchange. To take into account potential changes in the value of the collateral security, the cash lent would only amount to 90 to 95 percent of the market value of the security. Market jargon for this practice is that the security can be repoed with a haircut of 5 to 10 percent. I will not go into the mechanics of the repo market, but the resilience of this funding source, especially when the collateral posted was a securitised product, turned out to be poor contrary to the popular belief about its stability. That is, market participants such as money market funds did not differentiate loans collateralised by securitised products from uncollateralised loans when quality of this collateral came under scrutiny.

The risk of potential disruptions in dollar funding markets was underestimated even by large banks. A well-publicised example is the write-down amounting to $42.8 billion that UBS had to take between mid-2007 and mid-2008. The assets in question were mostly securitisation or resecuritisation products linked to warehoused assets or retained securitisations held in the trading book stemming from the originate-and-distribute business model. Retained securitisations were super senior AAA-rated tranches which simply could not be sold to market participants as they provided very little yield pick-up. Using the lower funding cost advantage for a large bank like UBS was the only way to hold on to these securitisation assets and generate a small profit from net interest income earned.

The trading desk at UBS responsible for managing these positions were of the opinion that these assets can either be sold in the market at their nominal price without any loss or alternatively the exposures can be hedged. These exposures denominated in US dollars were funded by raising interbank dollar deposits, issuing CDs mainly to US money market mutual funds and carrying out repo trades. Currency risk from unfunded exposures was hedged by entering into FX swaps. But when trust among financial market participants evaporated, interbank placements were withdrawn, repo markets backed by securitised assets shut down, and FX swap markets used to hedge currency risk became non-functional. A lack of understanding of the funding liquidity risks embedded in these positions led to the materialisation of large losses which only could be mitigated through state intervention.

Another area where multiple links existed and turned out to be a channel for financial contagion was the margining practices used in the over-the-counter derivatives trading business. Margining practices refer to the procedure followed by banks to mitigate counterparty risk when entering into bilateral derivatives trades with their clients. Such clients would normally include retail, institutional and hedge funds. Mitigation of counterparty risk was done by requiring clients to post an initial margin – technical term used for requesting collateral when a trade is negotiated – particularly when the client was liable under the derivatives contract to make a payment to the bank. This initial margin payment was collected in the form of government securities or cash to be paid into a custody account held at the investment bank. Almost 80 percent of the initial margins were paid in cash. The banks, on their part, never paid an initial margin to the client with the result that the client always had a counterparty risk exposure to the bank when engaging in derivatives trading.

There were exceptions to the above rule. When banks traded derivatives amongst themselves, they never posted initial margins. Insurance companies rated triple-A or double-A as well as a few large hedge funds negotiated deals with banks so that they also did not have to post initial margins. Beyond the requirements for most banking clients to post initial margins for derivatives trading, margining practices included another payment to be settled in cash and applicable to all counterparties in the derivatives trade. Specifically, banks examined the net exposures on all outstanding bilateral derivatives trades with a given counterparty around mid-day. This net exposure amount had to be paid by close of business the same day to the counterpart to whom this balance was due. This daily exchange of cash to bring the net exposures back to zero is called variation margin payments. But during the day before the cash settlement is made, large exposures can build up among banks involved in actively trading derivatives. Again there were exceptions to this rule with banks seldom paying variation margins to their smaller clients even if a banks' net exposure to the client went up.

Three sources of risk can be identified when counterparties engage in bilateral derivatives trading. Two stem from the solvency risk of a large bank actively engaged in providing services for derivatives trading based on bilateral contracts. The first source of risk arises from the variation margin payments that the bank has to make to other large banks given that there are no initial margin payments to provide collateral protection. A bank failing over a weekend would mean that the net exposures held by other banks on bilateral derivatives trades can only be recovered by becoming a general creditor in the bankruptcy proceedings of the failed bank, which can take months or even years.

Heightened counterparty risk, say to a large bank like UBS, will force the credit risk division of a bank to cut back on trading limits to UBS. In an interconnected market, many other banks will follow suit very soon when the news spreads. As a full service broker, the ability of UBS to offer derivatives trading to its clients will very much depend on whether it can offset risks by engaging in trades with other large universal or investment banks. Absent this capacity to offset risks, UBS will be come under severe pressure as unhedged risks on in its own balance sheet will start to grow.

A second source of risk linked to margining practices arises from exposures a client has to a bank resulting from the posting of initial margins. If the client had negotiated under the master agreement of the derivatives contract to have these initial and variation margin payments kept in a segregated client account, these funds can be reclaimed quickly. On the other hand, if the initial margin payments have been kept in a co-mingled account that includes many other clients, which was the case with Lehman Brothers, then the clients' funds have to be reclaimed under general bankruptcy procedures. Many hedge fund clients and asset managers faced lengthy court cases to reclaim their initial margin payments following the bankruptcy of Lehman Brothers. Awareness to these risks was simply not there in the run-up to the crisis.

A third source of risk, which is not related to the solvency of a bank, came from the practice of linking the requirement to pay initial margins with the credit rating of the counterparty. I mentioned earlier that insurance companies with triple-A ratings did not have to post initial margins with banks. Monoline insurers and general insurance companies were important providers of credit enhancement through default swaps to securitised assets so that they received higher ratings. The bilateral derivatives contracts that banks negotiated with insurers included a rating-trigger clause which required insurers to post initial margins when their ratings fell below double-A. These built-in rating triggers can cause very serious liquidity crisis for insurers. The government bailout of AIG was linked to this liquidity crisis when its credit rating fell below double-A to trigger large margin calls.

Beyond this, when the rating of the counterparty providing credit enhancement to securitised products and ABCP conduits gets downgraded, so do the ratings of those products and conduits. That can lead to selling pressures from money market mutual funds holding these assets as they may not meet the minimum credit rating requirements under US SEC regulation. All these were multiple links that existed in the run-up to the crisis.

The same channels of risk propagation also arise in repo trades executed with a bank. Additionally, the haircuts that were used on collateral posted on repo trades were also a source of problem. As I mentioned earlier, a haircut is simply a discount that is applicable to a security that is posted as collateral. A 5 percent haircut means that the security trading at a market price of $100 and posted as collateral will be discounted by 5 percent. The counterparty receiving this collateral from a bank on a repo trade will advance only $95 in cash. This discount is a form of protection against valuation and liquidity risk of the collateral if it has to be sold to recover the cash advanced to the bank. The haircuts negotiated by banks on securitised products were too low to mitigate loss in value under liquidation of such assets.

Two risk channels operated in the repo markets. One is when a client posts collateral assets comprising securitised products to a bank to receive cash. This practice was common among hedge funds that require prime broker financing to buy assets on leverage. When the credit rating of the securitised assets backed by subprime mortgages were downgraded and their prices fell, large increase in the haircuts on these securitises demanded by banks to their hedge fund clients forced them to liquidate these assets causing a downward price spiral. The second risk channel was banks on their part could not use these securitised assets as collateral in a repo trade with money market funds to raise cash because these assets did not meet money funds' minimum rating requirements anymore. The chain of bank credit intermediation was simply broken when a few links supporting this chain were damaged.

I discussed so far the multiple links that were created between financial market participants while pursuing the originate-and-distribute business model. This model allowed the flaws in the design of Basel II standards that gave capital relief when loans were shifted off-balance sheet to be fully exploited by banks. The mechanism employed by banks and mortgage originators was to extend housing loans to any willing borrower in the United States without doing proper due diligence of the borrowers' repayment capacity, and then selling these loans to off-balance sheet vehicles. The strategy was politically appealing as it served the American dream of home ownership. Because the roots of the financial crisis could be traced to the weak underwriting standards in the United States by extending mortgage loans to borrowers with weak or no credit history, which goes under the name subprime loans, the 2007–08 crisis is often referred to as the US subprime crisis.

Many of the linkages and channels through which the embedded risks in these mortgage loans materialised can also lead one to call this a US dollar funding crisis. Indeed, it was the lack of market access to dollar funding that gave this crisis a global character. Particularly, Asia was also drawn into the crisis despite banks there having no exposures to subprime mortgages. The channel through which this linkage happened was by sharp contraction in trade finance immediately following the Lehman bankruptcy. Trade finance refers to bank-intermediated credit extended either through loans or letters of credit and guarantees to firms to support international trade.

Global trade finance in 2008 exceeded $6 trillion comprising mostly short-term credit up to 3 months. In addition, trade finance has an important role in facilitating commodity trading with an estimated size of $1.5 trillion in revolving credit facilities. Commodity trade finance is mainly provided by large Swiss and French banks whereas for other forms of trade finance, more global banks are involved. But domestic banks in Asia are still the dominant providers of trade finance for local companies. The contraction in trade finance happened because nearly 80 percent of these financing arrangements are denominated in US dollars given that much of global trade is priced and settled in US dollars. Even when domestic banks were the main providers of trade credit, they relied on foreign banks to raise US dollars.

At least some of the collapse in global trade immediately after the Lehman bankruptcy – beyond those stemming from reduced global demand for goods – can be linked to the lack of access to dollar funding for banks extending trade finance credit. When global banks themselves faced dollar funding shortages with interbank markets dysfunctional, they had little incentive to lend dollars to other banks. The severity and the global reach of the financial crisis that stemmed from poor loan underwriting practices in the United States could have been reduced if the excessive reliance by banks in many jurisdictions on access to US dollar funding without adequate official backstop arrangements were recognised early and measures taken to mitigate them.

CHAPTER SEVEN

THE COMMITTEE

The BIS hosts a number of Committees that coordinate global policy on financial regulation. These Committees also provide a forum to exchange views on policy challenges and make assessments of emerging risks in financial markets that warrant attention. The role of the BIS in these Committees is to provide Secretariat support function for coordinating the work among member central banks and to prepare discussion papers for the Committees' deliberations. Much of the writing of policy documents or working group reports published by respective Committees is undertaken by the members of the Secretariat to the Committee. This function provides BIS a useful role in providing steer to the policy debates on financial regulation.

I was fortunate to be a Secretariat member of one of these Committees between 2006 and 2013, a period covering pre-crisis developments, crisis response and regulatory overhaul. This was the Committee on Global Financial System (CGFS) that monitors developments in global financial markets for central bank governors. The specific focus of the CGFS, henceforth referred to as the Committee, is to identify and assess potential sources of stress in global financial markets and to promote improvements to the functioning and stability of these markets.

I recall it was sometime in fall 2005 when my phone rang. When I picked up the phone I heard a familiar voice and was greeted with a blunt question. "What the hell are you doing in the banking department?" It was Stefan from the monetary and economics department whose lectures I had attended at the Basel University.

"Why, I am busy conducting workshops and advising central banks on risk and reserve management policies," I told him.

"Look, we need someone who understands the financial markets jargon and can communicate this in simple English to senior central bankers by preparing discussion notes," he said. "The CGFS Secretariat performs this function, and I would very much wish to have you in the team."

I always enjoyed doing different things in life, and when a new opportunity came knocking on my door, I could not refuse. Already in late 2005 I was allowed to attend the discussions of the Committee so that I will be better prepared for the task of drafting discussion notes for the meetings.

My first assignment in the Committee work was to support a study group tasked to examine factors that were contributing to subdued volatility in financial markets beginning about mid-2004. Periods of low volatility support banks' ability and willingness to extend more credit. This is because market risk capital requirements are lower when volatility is low so that banks' balance sheet capacity is increased. In addition, hedging costs to offset risks are lower for banks in such periods. Sustained periods of low volatility also induce market participants to take more risk. This happens through lower margin requirements for derivatives exposures and lower haircuts on collateral assets that allow greater leverage to be employed by hedge funds. A sudden spike in volatility following a reversal in market sentiment from unexpected news can have implications for financial stability as risk bearing capacity from the channels noted here is sharply curtailed. Financial press often depicts the level of volatility in stock markets as a measure of fear or risk aversion in markets.

The assessment made by the study group when reporting to the Committee was that the reduction in volatility had been associated with improved financial conditions. They included, increased market liquidity, greater role of institutional investors in providing financial protection through derivatives, better communication from central banks to financial market participants, and stronger company balance sheets resulting from lower leverage and improved earnings.

The study group also drew some interesting conclusions why volatility in the US interest rate markets remains subdued. This is important because volatility spillovers often flow from the US markets to other financial centres. The group specifically focused on US mortgage markets, which subsequently turned out to be the transmitter of volatility shocks. Let me elaborate on this as the Committee was briefed in May 2006 on these developments, and one can raise the question as to whether early signs of build-up of tensions in this market segment were missed.

Among the many unique features of the US mortgage markets, one is the granting of the option to borrowers to prepay their mortgage loans early when interest rates fall, and then to refinance them at lower rates. By granting this "call option" to borrowers, investors in the mortgage-backed securities forgo the benefit of making profits in a falling interest rate environment. (Prices of conventional bonds rise when interest rates fall). Large investors like Fannie Mae and Freddie Mac will try to position themselves to profit from falling interest rates by entering into dynamic hedging strategies.

In a dynamic hedging strategy, mortgage agencies will buy US Treasuries if they expect interest rates to fall, and sell these holdings if they expect interest rates to rise. Given the balance sheet size of mortgage agencies, such dynamic hedging strategies tend to amplify price movements and add to volatility in the US interest rate market. But towards late 2003, the volume of trades linked to dynamic hedging declined materially with expectations that US interest rates will be on an upward trajectory. This lowered hedging-induced volatility and at the same time mortgage refinancing activities fell when interest rates started rising in 2004.

Three other developments happened in that period. One was the large increase in foreign exchange reserves that I mentioned in an earlier chapter while at the same time outstanding US Treasuries declined or rose only very slowly. This prompted a number of Asian central banks to buy US mortgage-backed securities. As buy-and-hold investors, they did not hedge the interest rate exposures held on the central bank balance sheets. A second development was the compression of term premium in interest rates in many advanced economies. Term premium is the compensation that investors require for the risk that their forecasts of future short-term rates will prove to be incorrect. Improved and more forward-looking central bank communication on monetary policy reduced the level of uncertainty of future short-term rates leading to lower volatility in term premium, which has a direct effect on long-term interest rate volatility.

A third factor was a shift from issuance of fixed-rate to adjustable-rate mortgage loans, which increased from having a share of 10 percent in 2003 to 30 percent in early 2006 in the newly originated mortgage loans. Investors holding these adjustable-rate mortgages were not exposed to interest rate risk on their balance sheet that required hedging. That said the interest rate risk was being shifted to households when they took such loans. This happens because the interest payments are linked to the short-term rates set by the central bank, and when this rises, so do interest payments that are due. With benefit of hindsight, it turned out households were ill-prepared to shoulder this risk due to poor underwriting practices and also because mortgage originators did not explain the embedded risks in such loans to borrowers properly.

None of the above developments, which were reported to the Committee, meant the observed trends in low financial markets volatility were a source of major concern for financial stability requiring policy intervention. While there was recognition that the low levels of volatility may not be sustained, reversal to higher and more normal levels of market volatility was not expected to disrupt market functioning.

Developments in US mortgage markets as well as in securitisation products were still debated in the Committee as to whether risks are being appropriately priced by investors. There was clearly a desire to understand the financial engineering behind some of these securitisation and resecuritisation products rated triple-A which provided sometimes 2 percent yield pickup over US Treasuries. I was assigned the task to explain the financial engineering behind some such products to the Committee through an easy-to-read discussion note for a meeting in November 2006.

My task was anything but easy as I decided to pick a new structured credit product that was introduced in the market known as the constant proportion debt obligation (CPDO). Rated as AAA by a major rating agency, it offered investors 2 percent yield pick up over the interbank offer rate. The yield pickup was also similar over a comparable maturity triple-A rated corporate bonds. In contrast to collateralised debt obligations, the structuring in a CPDO was done on the asset side of the SPV balance sheet using a variable leverage and dynamic hedging strategy rather than through tranching of claims on the liability side that is common with securitisation products. I will not get into the details of the structuring and credit risk modelling involved, but the discussion note raised the awareness of many members of the Committee that they simply cannot keep up with the financial innovation that was going on. There was a feeling that complexity of these new products was complicating risk assessment.

Early signs of trouble in the US mortgage market started showing up already in the beginning of 2007. In February 2007, HSBC announced that it will take a credit loss of $10.5 billion on its US subprime loans. The bank attributed this loss to a failure of its risk models to predict much higher borrower defaults on adjustable-rate mortgages due to lack of historical data. That is, the banks' view was that the increase in US policy rates from 1 percent in June 2004 to 5.25 percent in July 2006 was unprecedented, and that they could not correctly predict its impact on borrowers' capacity to service their mortgage loans.

But HSBC was not alone in reporting losses on mortgage loans. Already in January 2007 Washington Mutual reported losses in the fourth quarter of 2006 stemming from rising delinquencies in subprime loans. Other mortgage lenders like New Century Financial and US Bancorp also faced similar challenges. All these players were among the largest underwriters of US subprime mortgage loans.

These developments did not go unnoticed in the Committee with a mandate to monitor and report to central bank governors global market developments that can have adverse effects on financial conditions. But to some extent it was seen as a necessary adjustment and consistent with the goal of the US Federal Reserve to apply brakes on mortgage loan growth by raising policy rates in a measured way and communicated to market participants in a transparent manner.

For many who are outsiders to Wall Street, a lingering question in their minds would be, "Why did mortgage originators and banks not take action to scale back loan growth when the US Federal Reserve made its intensions clear already in early 2004 to raise interest rates?" The answer lies in the incentive structure underlying the originate-and-distribute model that I drew attention to earlier. Revenues to banks underwriting these loans were fee-based and did not rely on the net interest margins that could be generated by retaining these loans on balance sheet and managing risks associated with them. Changing incentive structures will require changing regulation. This cannot be done in few months or even in few years' time.

This period also witnessed dramatic growth in leveraged finance that I had mentioned earlier, which refers to corporate debt with relatively high credit risk. At its March 2007 meeting, the Committee setup a working group to investigate the role, importance and characteristics of the various market participants in the functioning of leveraged finance markets to gain insight into the channels through which a disruption in these markets could impact financial stability.

The Committee's discussions in May 2007 explored the adverse impact developments in US mortgage markets can have in other jurisdictions. Spanish mortgage lending that had also seen large growth over this period was a candidate for some scrutiny. But there was reassurance from Bank of Spain that banks were obliged to do "dynamic provisioning" for loan losses that had a forward-looking element to determine appropriate provisions, and the loan underwriting standards were stricter. These, in their view, reassured markets that the Spanish banking system is sound even if losses were to materialise.

The focus on risks still remained more firmly on US mortgage markets in the first half of 2007. To provide some insights on potential losses that investors may be facing by holding products backed by US subprime loans, the discussion note for the Committee included price developments in market indices used to benchmark performance of such products. Because the liquidity in the cash markets for these products was poor, index providers used prices in derivatives markets to construct the benchmarks. That is, instead of using the US subprime loan securitisations, the traded prices of credit default swaps referencing these securitisations with major banks serving as market makers were used. These indices, introduced in January 2006, went by the name ABX.HE to indicate that the assets backing these derivative indices were subprime home equity loans. There were several of these sub-indices each referencing a specific rating category as well as time period over which these loans were granted.

The price developments based on these indices showed that from July 2006 to May 2007 there was no deterioration in market sentiment for triple-A, double-A or single-A rated tranches of securitisations backed by US subprime loans that were issued during the first six months of 2006. That is, market participants using these indices to either hedge risk or to provide default protection had not changed their pricing policies to signal that credit risks for subprime loans were now higher. Considering that the holdings of the subprime assets were widely dispersed among different financial market participants, some members of the Committee felt that even price falls by 10 to 15 percent in these indices over the course of the year it would not create material risks to financial stability.

This conclusion was based on roughly the following reasoning. By some measures the amount of poor quality subprime loans could be about $750 billion. Suppose the prices fell by 10 to 15 percent, they would signal about $100 billion loss on these exposures, but by no means these sums are large enough to disrupt global financial markets when holdings are widely distributed. Indeed, it is not uncommon for the American stock market to lose $0.5 trillion in value during a week when risks are elevated. The Committee felt that closer monitoring of developments in the US subprime market is warranted, but there was a clear recognition that risks in the financial system were rising.

What I noticed during these discussions was an increased concern among central banks in Europe about developments in the US subprime markets relative to their US counterparts. That was because of the exposures to these assets many European banks held in their balance sheets, which were still rated as high quality and attracting very low capital charges under Basel II. Many who are not familiar with central bank communication policy would wonder why they did not sound alarms if they had concerns about the embedded risks in these exposures. The reason is that subprime loans were originated in the United States and flagging concerns about their quality or risks they posed would be the prerogative of the Federal Reserve as per central bank code of conduct.

The general feeling I had after the weekend meetings held in Basel is that some risks in the US mortgage market may unwind soon resulting is losses to various players. It was not so much as to whether but rather when and how big the losses will be when risks materialise. If you were not a central banker, you had the freedom to raise concerns openly about rising risks that the press might pick up. It was easy to point to risk build-up in the US subprime markets and blame weak underwriting practices for it. And then to conclude that if tail risks were to materialise, the losses can be large – which is what a credit loss distribution function will tell you. A hedge fund managing client money can position itself to make large profits if this scenario materialises. Speculating and taking risks is their job. Some win and many lose. But a central banker has to identify the specific channels through which the risks will materialise and the mechanisms that may amplify it so that mitigating actions can be taken.

One did not have to wait a full summer to see the materialisation of the risks in the subprime market. In July, two hedge funds sponsored by Bear Stearns and invested heavily in US subprime securitisations failed with little recovery value left for investors. On 6 August 2007, American Home Mortgage Investment Corporation filed for Chapter 11 bankruptcy leading to a term extension on outstanding ABCP issued by one of its funding conduits. A few days later, BNP Paribas announced that it will suspend withdrawal of money from three funds invested in the US subprime assets with funds totalling $3.8 billion. The reason it cited was its inability to appropriately value the investments in subprime assets in the prevailing market environment.

Already in the first week of August, the German bank IKB had reported large losses from subprime exposures. It was the classic example of risks from multiple links that I highlighted in the previous chapter. IKB had setup an off-balance sheet conduit called Rheinland Funding in tax-havens to which it provided liquidity support. The conduit, which held significant share of subprime loans on the asset side, was funded on the liability side by selling ABCP backed by subprime assets to US money market funds and other investors.

The conduit received credit commitments from Deutsche Bank which appears to have been structured to be unconditionally cancellable to benefit from lower capital charges under Basel II. When Deutsche Bank withdrew credit support at the time the conduit faced difficulties to roll over maturing ABCP debt in view of rising risks in the subprime market, the house of cards fell apart. The German bank needed a rescue package of €3.5 billion supported by the state and other credit unions to remain solvent. Problems linked to subprime mortgage exposures also surfaced in UBS, a large Swiss bank. These early signs of trouble confirmed why central bankers in Europe were so nervous about mortgage market developments across the Atlantic starting already in late 2006.

The state rescue of the German bank in the second week of August 2007 set the timeline for start of the global financial crisis. Capital positions of other European banks with substantial US subprime exposure came under scrutiny by investors. But the immediate reaction of US money market funds and investors in short-term bank debt and ABCP markets was to drastically scale back the permissible credit limits for buying these assets. The outstanding volume of ABCP started a steep decline from mid-August to December 2007. This had large funding implications for banks that sponsored conduits or SIVs issuing such paper as their credit commitments to provide liquidity got activated.

The September 2007 meeting of the Committee reviewed these developments. The discussions were now more focused on what policy responses are needed to manage the risks and limit contagion. Injecting liquidity into the interbank markets was seen as the first response to mitigate rising tensions in funding markets. But there was unease that a large bank in the United Kingdom was facing trouble. Most knew which bank that was, but the extent of the problem was not known. Later that week television cameras showed long lines in front of the various branches of Northern Rock, the British bank specialising in mortgage financing, wanting to withdraw their deposits. News flashed that there is a traditional depositor bank run considering that only £2,000 of deposits was fully protected. The story is much more complex, and I will return to the Northern Rock case in the next chapter as it revealed important lessons for policy when central banks went back to redesign the financial architecture.

The Committees' work already switched to a fact-finding mode to support and coordinate central bank responses by September 2007. One area where there was broad consensus was in trying to understand the shortcomings in the models used by credit rating agencies to rate securitisation and resecuritisation products. Already in June and July 2007, Moody's and Standard and Poor's downgraded the credit ratings of a large volume of securitisation products backed by subprime mortgages. This had knock-on effects on ratings of both monoline insurers providing credit protection for such products as well as on ABCP conduits and SIVs that held these assets. These were the early triggers for subsequent panic in the markets beginning in August that I highlighted above.

To understand the ratings process that resulted in these sudden and large downgrades of subprime securitisations, the Committee organised meetings with credit ratings agencies and with investors that use ratings of securitised products for investment decisions. Subsequently, a study group was established to suggest recommendations to alter existing practices in rating these products, including disclosures to investors on important input parameters used by credit agencies that influence rating outcomes. I had the privilege to participate in these roundtables and also serve as Secretary to the study group.

The study group's findings provided important insights into the reasons for the poor performance of the rating agency models. Specifically, the accuracy of credit ratings of securitised products backed by mortgage loans depend crucially on the precision of economic forecasts that influence house prices. But rating agencies reported that an increased willingness of borrowers to simply walk away from mortgage debt contributed to extraordinary levels of early default that the models could not predict. This was linked to deterioration in underwriting standards, which rating agencies failed to spot early on resulting in underestimation of the probability of default as well as the propensity for multiple defaults. A factor that influenced the large rating downgrades on securitised products as revealed by rating agencies was the dramatic change in their outlook for US housing markets in 2007. Whereas in January 2007 they expected nationwide house price indices not to decline during the market downturn, they revised this to a 10 percent decline in June 2007, and subsequently to 20 percent decline in January 2008.

Separately, the working group on leveraged finance setup by the Committee discussed many of the developments taking place in the second half of 2007 and provided its risk assessment on on-going developments in that market segment. With investors becoming more risk averse, syndicated loans made on firm commitment basis to fund leveraged buyout transactions could not be distributed to end-investors as intended. Many banks that were arrangers of these loans had to take them on their balance sheet and fund it. Because this increased their needs for dollar funding, US banks scaled back their activities in the FX swap market resulting in US dollar funding shortages to European banks. German, French and Swiss banks were most affected through their trade finance activities and exposures to US mortgage assets. To provide US dollars to banks in Europe, the Federal Reserve entered into currency swap arrangement with the ECB and the Swiss National Bank in second week of December 2007.

The collapse of Bear Stearns in mid-March 2008 and its subsequent sale to JP Morgan Chase delivered the final blow for investors still holding US subprime securitisations. The following month UBS recognised significant additional losses on its subprime holdings. Suddenly, the market had lost confidence in credit rating agencies and securitisation products. Still, the elephant in the room was the US mortgage agencies that held significant share of these subprime assets. There were some direct questions to the Federal Reserve representatives during May 2008 Committee meeting from central banks holding large exposures to these agencies either through the unsecured debt issued by the agencies or through the mortgage-backed securities guaranteed by them. That is, central banks wanted to know how the dividing line between implicit and explicit government guarantees for mortgage agencies should be interpreted. The US response gave at least some reassurance to central banks that were exposed to these mortgage agencies through their foreign exchange reserves holdings.

In the first half of 2008, I did not observe much worry from Asian central banks about the health of their banking systems given no or only limited exposures held to US subprime assets. That changed in September when Lehman Brothers was allowed to fail. The events that took place during this fateful month including a run on US money market funds and government bailout of AIG a few days after Lehman failure have been documented and explained by many. I will therefore not discuss this here. But the events that followed leading to a complete freeze of market-making activities provided many lessons to central banks. The Committee provided a strong voice to various other Basel forums for reforming the financial architecture by doing a post-mortem of the inherent flaws that contributed to the crisis by establishing a number of working groups. I will discuss the policy lessons in the next chapter which contributed to far-reaching financial reforms.

Before I conclude this chapter, let me try to answer the question I raised in the earlier chapter, namely how much central bankers were aware of the weak links in the financial architecture that would ultimately collapse. My own recollection is that the importance of some of the links I had discussed earlier was underestimated. I draw this conclusion based on the time that was spent discussing these channels of risk propagation. For example, the role of haircuts as an amplification mechanism when banks moved increasingly to repo-based funding and the risks from margining practices on derivatives trading were both underestimated during the early phase of the risk build-up.

That said, even if these risk channels had been identified earlier, the main policy intervention instrument that could be used from 2004 was raising interest rates, which the Federal Reserve did. Central banks simply did not have the powers to intervene in private bilateral contracts among financial participants which would alter either the margining practices on derivatives trades or the eligible assets they could accept as collateral on repo trades as well as the applicable haircuts on them. Risk weights to be used on securitisation assets held by banks under Basel II were already legislated and supervisors only had the discretion to impose more capital requirements under Pillar 2. These were not areas where readymade central bank policy toolkits could be employed, and intervening in this area would have needed a change in regulation.

In the aftermath of the financial crisis, some have argued that the Federal Reserve could have exercised its powers under the Home Ownership and Equity Protection Act of 1994 to restrict predatory lending practices in granting of subprime loans. That is possible, but I cannot recall any central banker raising this issue and I am not aware of what constraints there were to exercise those powers under the Act.

With benefit of hindsight, what I think was not examined or analysed properly by the Committee, and by implication by central banks, is the extent of reliance by banks and other market players on the access to and the resilience of cross border US dollar funding that only became apparent in the fall of 2007. Letting cross-border funding risks to build-up was a costly mistake as early identification of this risk might have reduced the severity and global impact of the financial crisis by taking mitigating actions. For that reason I like to call this not just a US subprime crisis but also a US dollar funding crisis.

Many readers might wonder why I did not discuss the build-up of risks in the balance sheets of US mortgage agencies, and why the Federal Reserve did not intervene early to take corrective actions. The simple answer is that the Federal Reserve did not have the mandate to do this. The US Congress created a two-part regulatory structure in 1992 to monitor Fannie Mae and Freddie Mac for compliance with their statutory mission and to limit their risk-taking. The Office of Federal Housing Enterprises Oversight (OFHEO) was setup in 1992 as an independent agency within US Department of Housing and Urban Development as the safety-and-soundness regulator.

The mortgage agencies had a line of credit with the US Treasury, which was interpreted by market participants as a signal of implicit government guarantee. Risk-based capital requirements for mortgage agencies were set by statute at very low levels, and OFHEO lacked the authority to adjust them. Moreover, OFHEO was subject to annual Congressional appropriations process and through this susceptible to political interference.

As of June 2008, the combined on-balance sheet assets held by Fannie Mae and Freddie Mac were $1.7 trillion, and an additional $3.7 trillion of agency mortgage-backed securities were guaranteed by them. The total equity of the two agencies that supported this risk exposure amounted to $54 billion. If we pick a risk weight of 35 percent for the assets that were held or guaranteed, a bank with this balance sheet exposure would have had a capital ratio of 2.8 percent under Basel II. This is far below the minimum capital requirement of 8 percent of risk-weighted assets under Basel standards. If market risk and operational risk capital requirements would be included, the capital ratio would be even lower than 2.8 percent. On 7 September 2008, both mortgage agencies went into conservatorship under the newly established Federal Housing Finance Agency, and the US Treasury injected $187 billion funds through preferred stock to restore capital positions.

To sum up, the Federal Reserve had powers to take the punch bowl away from a Wall Street party, but it did not have the same powers when the US Congress had a party. It also did not have the mandate to regulate Swiss, German and French banks and to instruct them to de-risk their exposures to securitisations backed by US subprime loans. But it had one tool, namely control of domestic interest rates to make borrowing expensive for US households so that they will not be able to afford financing new mortgage loans. That it did. And the non-recourse nature of the mortgage loans ensured that the financing risks became someone else's problem.

CHAPTER EIGHT

POLICY LESSONS

Next time it will be different. This is perhaps true of every crisis. Yet, a deep crisis provides opportunities to rewire the financial architecture rather than to simply replace the fuses that had blown. But to do that regulators have to do a post mortem of the crisis to identify market practices that trigger adverse feedback and contribute to financial instability. Some may recall that the failure of one rubber O-ring designed to separate the sectors of the rocket booster led to the Space Shuttle Challenger disaster. If the temperature during the night before launch had been 10 degrees Celsius warmer, the disaster could have been avoided. In life, we often tend to focus on complex linkages to build fail-safe systems. But on many occasions failures are caused by constructs that we think are less important for the overall safety. The financial system is not an exception to this rule.

Many good books have been written on the causes and consequences of the financial crisis and each of them provide different prescriptions on how to build safer financial systems based on the identified weaknesses. This reminds me of a story I heard as a child about four blind people who were taken to an elephant and asked to identify the object. The blind man who feels the leg says it is a pillar; the one who grabs the tail says it is a rope; the one who feels the trunk says it is a branch of a tree; and the one who feels the ear says it is a husking basket. I am aware that I risk becoming the fifth blind person examining the elephant and concluding something else. I will leave the judgement to the readers.

One advantage I can claim to have over many others is that I waited nearly 10 years before presenting the post mortem of the crisis. But to provide an objective assessment, I will try to supress the urge to give my personal views on the constructs that caused the crisis as it can be biased. What I will present as policy lessons in this chapter is to a large extent based on discussions and debates that took place among senior central bankers that I had access to while they analysed the weaknesses of the regulatory regime that contributed to this deep crisis. I will deal with the responses to these policy lessons in the subsequent chapters.

As I already discussed in the earlier chapters, there were multiple players, multiple links and multiple causes for the financial crisis. Yet, a pervasive theme that runs through every informed analysis of the crisis is the extensive interconnectedness and interdependencies among different players in the financial system. If I had to single out one important policy lesson learned, I would highlight the need to dismantle this interconnectedness in the financial system.

To draw lessons for policy, I will discuss the failures of specific financial institutions, and in some cases, a system of financial institutions to highlight the deficiencies in the financial architecture that caused the crisis. Many elements of the weak links contributing to the crisis were already discussed in the earlier chapters. While some repetition of these links is difficult to avoid, I will try to ensure that they help to focus attention on the channels through which the crisis occurred so that readers will be able to appreciate why certain financial sector reforms were introduced.

For the benefit of readers who may not be familiar with balance sheets, let me begin with some information on the composition of bank balance sheets. Let us assume that the bank has assets worth $100 million. These assets usually comprise loans to the non-financial sector, retail and commercial mortgage loans, loans to small businesses, and some cash and government bonds. On the liability side, also worth $100 million, the bank will have retail bank deposits, uncollateralised short and medium-term bonds issued by the bank, and other short or medium-term liabilities that are backed by collateral. If these liabilities add up to $95 million, the residual $5 million will be bank equity. The relative share of the different liabilities a bank issues will provide insights on the business model and the type of the bank – that is, whether it is structured to operate more as a retail bank or as an investment bank.

With this information clarified, let me begin with the failure of the Northern Rock which had practically no exposure to US subprime mortgages. As a mortgage bank, Northern Rock was in the business of prime mortgage lending to UK households. Yet, what made it different from other UK mortgage banks was its greater reliance on non-retail funding. The share of retail deposits comprised about 23 percent of its funding liabilities in the first half of 2007. Non-retail funding comprising interbank deposits, unsecured debt and other customer deposits amounted to about 26 percent of liabilities. Collateralised debt comprising covered bonds and securitisation notes accounted for 7.5 and 43.5 percent of the funding liabilities. Being backed by good quality prime UK mortgage collateral at a time when UK house prices were rising and unemployment was low, Northern Rock had little difficulties issuing medium and long-term collateralised debt until 2006.

For a mortgage bank, Northern Rock's greater reliance on capital market funding was necessitated by its rapid growth in assets. Between June 1998 and June 2007 its assets grew from about 17 billion pounds to 113 billion pounds. It simply could not expand its branch-based retail depositor base to keep up with this asset growth. To increase deposit funding, Northern Rock pursued the strategy of offering postal accounts as well as offshore and internet banking accounts which together comprised 75 percent of the retail deposit funding.

In the pre-crisis period, Basel regulatory standards focused primarily on the asset side of the balance sheet. There were no rules providing guidance on how the assets of a bank will have to be funded. In general, when a bank funds its assets predominantly by raising retail deposits – which is what retail banks and mortgage banks normally do – adequate levels of deposit insurance coverage and proper regulatory oversight ensures that the bank's funding base remains stable. By contrast, banks that rely more on investment banking activities tend to have a larger share of funding in capital markets. Indeed, it has been customary to tell a banks' business model by examining the composition of its liabilities.

The increased reliance on capital market funding of investment banks is supported by the greater share of tradable assets held by such banks. Some of the trading assets held are funded in repo markets, but a significant share of wholesale funding of large investment or universal banks comprises unsecured debt. Yet, investment banks manage their funding liquidity risks by holding adequate share of assets that are eligible for repo operations with the central bank. Northern Rock's funding structure resembled that of a universal bank with large investment banking business but with a slight modification namely, of relying excessively – to the extent of 50 percent – on securitised debt and covered bonds. While such funding structures are observed among some Nordic mortgage banks, this creates asset encumbrance – meaning that a large share of the bank assets are not accessible to unsecured creditors under insolvency. To mitigate the risk that access to unsecured funding markets might be lost, liquidity insurance policies become essential. Northern Rock has very little of this.

Let me illustrate the problem arising from asset encumbrance to unsecured creditors with an example. Suppose a bank with $100 worth of assets is funded with $48 of collateralised debt, $24 of uncollateralised debt, $24 of retail deposits and $4 of equity. Depending on the level of overcollateralization required to achieve a desired credit rating for the collateralised debt, about $54 worth of assets will typically be encumbered. That is, these assets will not be available to meet creditor claims belonging to the category of retail deposits and unsecured debtholders. In addition, if the collateralised debt has recourse to the banks' balance sheet, as is the case for covered bonds, these bondholders become claimants in the residual assets of the bank with the same rank as the retail depositors and senior unsecured creditors.

One can infer from the above example that as the share of collateralised funding in a banks' balance sheet rises, the potential recovery values for unsecured creditors becomes lower. When concerns about a banks' creditworthiness rises, unsecured debtholders are often the first to run. This usually happens when prudent risk management practices pursued by the credit risk department of institutional investors result in a reduction in permissible exposures to the bank. When a short-term unsecured debt of the bank matures, institutional investors will not be able to reinvest in the banks' debt if credit limits are withdrawn. Northern Rock faced such a bank run – not in the classical style of depositor withdrawals but in the form of institutional investors not rolling over their maturing short- and medium-term unsecured debt. Interbank deposits are also subject to similar runs. What made Northern Rocks' funding strategy very risky was that, unlike investment banks, it did not hold assets that were normally repo eligible with Bank of England, and consequently, making it vulnerable to loss of market-based funding. That is, it did not pursue adequate funding liquidity insurance policies.

But why were institutional investors worried considering that most of Northern Rock's lending was backed by prime quality UK mortgage assets? The answer lies both in the investor base that Northern Rock was tapping to raise unsecured short-term debt as well as in the share of assets that were encumbered. Out of £101 billion of total assets as of December 2006, the amount of encumbered assets was £55 billion which was backing £46.2 billion of collateralised debt. The total equity amounted to £3.2 billion. The balance sheet as of December 2006 also shows a notional foreign currency derivatives exposure of £44 billion implemented mainly through FX swaps. While the net exposure will be lower, the FX swap transactions suggest that a sizable share of outstanding debt was issued in foreign currency with short-term unsecured debt targeting US institutional investors that included money market mutual funds.

In a period when US subprime mortgages came under scrutiny, there will be a general tendency to restrict credit limits to banks having a significant share of mortgage assets without regard to where they were originated. Beyond this, any prudent risk management department that examines the December 2006 balance sheet of Northern Rock would also be concerned about the amount of subordination of unsecured debt through asset encumbrance. As I noted earlier, this depresses the potential recovery values on unsecured debt under bankruptcy, particularly when the equity share is only 3 percent of liabilities. Retrenchment of unsecured funding will set off a chain reaction with interbank deposits taking flight particularly when a bank has limited options to forestall funding stress, and finally when retail depositors queue up to get their money back, a bank run will be unavoidable. This in a nutshell is what happened to Northern Rock.

The Northern Rock episode provided important lessons for regulatory policy. It became evident when the post-mortem was done that banking regulation narrowly focused on the asset side of the balance sheet – as Basel II did – was not sufficient to ensure that a solvent bank, as seen from the capital requirements perspective, can remain operational when faced with funding problems. Being also resilient to funding stress required regulation to be prescriptive about how the liability side of the bank balance sheet should be structured. The demise of Northern Rock provided key insights to regulators when they went about designing liquidity regulation to complement capital regulation under the revised Basel III standards.

The Northern Rock failure was also a forerunner for policy debates about how problem banks can be resolved without committing taxpayer money. The corporate restructuring done by invoking Chapter 11 bankruptcy proceedings in the United States, for example, simply does not work for restructuring banks. This is because there is moratorium on interest and debt repayments so that creditors cannot access their funds until the restructuring operation is completed. It is not prudent to impose a moratorium on withdrawal of demand deposits held by retail and other clients. Furthermore, bank restructuring or resolution requires close involvement of regulators rather than creditors as is the case for corporate restructurings.

Technically, Northern Rock could have been put into administration – a term used when a bank is declared to be insolvent and creditor claims are met through lengthy bankruptcy proceeding. That would have triggered the bank guarantee fund to pay out to depositors £2,000 which was fully insured. Beyond this, 90 percent of deposits up to £35,000 were insured. Depositor claims that exceeded this sum as well as unsecured debtholder claims would be repaid on a pro rata basis following a strict creditor hierarchy from the liquidation value of Northern Rock's assets that are not encumbered. As this procedure can last a few years, confidence in the UK banking system could be undermined causing more panic. Moreover, the securitisation scheme Northern Rock used also posed problems for orderly winding down of the bank. The UK authorities simply could not risk exercising the option of putting Northern Rock into administration. The importance of having an effective bank resolution regime to deal with non-viable banks was another a key policy lesson learned from the Northern Rock episode.

The demise of the US investment bank Bear Stearns and its takeover by JP Morgan in March 2008 provided very different sets of policy lessons from that of Northern Rock. Many of Bear Stearns problems can be traced back to the two hedge funds it sponsored through its subsidiary, Bear Stearns Asset Management. Both hedge funds were highly leveraged and were investing in high-grade securitisation products backed by US subprime mortgage assets. By end-2006 the two funds held more than $20 billion worth of securities.

The trigger for the problems that surfaced in the two hedge funds was the rating downgrade of securitised products backed by subprime mortgages in early 2007 that led to repricing of these assets. The significant leverage held by the hedge funds was generated by collateralised borrowing in repo markets using these securitised products. A price fall of these assets creates large margin calls, and the Bear Stearns hedge funds were unable to meet them in June 2007. To avoid reputational damage, Bear Stearns injected a collateralised loan worth $1.5 billion into one of the funds. For the second fund, Merrill Lynch took possession of $850 million of repo collateral and tried to sell them in the market when margins calls were not met. But as the liquidation values were too low, only $100 million of these assets were reportedly sold. The price discovery for these securitised products generated by the asset sales eventually led to the wind up of the two hedge funds in July 2007 with little residual value for investors.

To avoid repetition, I will skip developments that took place in the second half of 2007, which I had discussed in the previous chapter. As the market for securitised products backed by US subprime assets became illiquid in the first quarter of 2008, Bear Stearns that held a large portfolio of these assets faced problems funding them. Because Bear Stearns did not have access to the discount window of the Federal Reserve due to it being a nondepository financial institution, the funding stress intensified. Eventually, Bear Stearns was taken over by JP Morgan, a process that was coordinated by the Federal Reserve.

Focusing on policy, the collapse of Bear Stearns in March 2008 can be linked to two developments. One is the continued fall in prices of securitised products backed by subprime assets that resulted in significant increase in margin calls as they were used in repo-based funding. The other was that hedge fund clients who were using Bear Stearns for prime brokerage services started transferring their prime brokerage accounts to other investment banks causing further liquidity drains. What the hedge funds were trying to do was to reduce the counterparty exposure to Bear Stearns arising from the posting of collateral and the custody of securities held in their brokerage account.

Let me now summarise two main lessons learned from the collapse of Bear Stearns that influenced regulatory policy. One was how financial leverage was being created by market participants, and what the policy goal is for how this should be created to safeguard financial stability. The second lesson links directly to how much financial leverage banks should be allowed to take to mitigate build-up of excessive risks in the financial system. Let me elaborate on each of them below.

I had mentioned earlier that the hedge funds Bear Stearns sponsored were highly leveraged. What was known is that investor funds amounted to about $1.5 billion but the total size of securities' exposure held was close to $20 billion. Leverage, which amplifies gains and losses arising from market movements, can be taken either through the derivatives market or the cash market. If done through the cash market, a hedge fund would ask its prime broker to provide a collateralised loan to buy the securities it wants to hold, which the broker will then keep as collateral. These transactions go under the name repo trades. Investment banks also create leverage by engaging in repo-based funding. Money market funds often provide such funding by being the counterparty to the repo trades.

By engaging in collateralised lending, a creditor can more easily recover the money lent by simply liquidating the collateral assets held as opposed to going through a lengthy bankruptcy proceeding when lending is uncollateralised. A prudent lender would take the collateral asset at sufficient discount to ensure that there will be no loss if the collateral has to be liquidated even in adverse market conditions. In mortgage financing, prudent banks usually lend only 70 percent of the value of the house which serves as collateral, and the rest of the amount has to be self-financed. In this case, we can talk about the haircut on the mortgage collateral to be 30 percent.

Imposing a haircut on the market value of a collateral asset transforms a risky asset into a safe asset. A safe asset is one for which there will be willing buyers at the quoted price. If you want to sell your 10 years old car, a dozen buyers will line up at your door if you offer it at a deep discount relative to the market price for the car. Large discounts transform an illiquid and risky asset into a safe and liquid asset. Banks and prime brokers routinely lend money by taking traded equities as collateral by transforming them into safe assets by imposing a 20 percent haircut on them. That is, if a stock is trading today at $100 per share, the bank will take the stock as collateral and lend $80 to the counterparty. The actual haircut will vary depending on the creditworthiness of the counterparty.

Returning to the hedge funds sponsored by Bear Stearns, with $1.5 billion investor money, these funds were able to raise collateralised borrowing worth $18.5 billion to reach an exposure amounting to $20 billion. A simple calculation will show that the average repo haircuts on the predominantly securitisation assets held by the funds should have been around 8 percent. For some highly rated securitisation products it was perhaps even as low as 4 percent as the hedge funds would have had to retain some liquidity to meet margin calls. Had the repo haircuts been more prudent and set at 20 percent, the leverage that could have been taken would be much lower with total securities exposure limited to about $7 billion.

The problem with setting haircuts too low for non-government securities is that when market liquidity conditions change, the posted collateral may no longer serve as a safe asset to the creditor. To mitigate this risk, the creditor may either raise the applicable haircuts or simply cut back on the credit limits to the lender. This can set into motion adverse dynamics for financial stability. These factors were at play which contributed to the failure of the hedge funds as well as the subsequent bailout of Bear Stearns.

The policy intervention needed to address this market failure that contributes to procyclical leverage dynamics was to ensure that the posted collateral securities qualify as safe assets in all states of the world. That requires setting minimum level of haircuts for different assets, which will have to be maintained through the business cycle and calibrated to periods of stressed market conditions. The revised Basel standards implemented this policy goal through capital regulation for collateralised exposures, which I will elaborate in the next chapter.

The second lesson learned from the Bear Stearns bailout was that constraints on permissible leverage should complement capital regulation. Prior to bailout, Bear Stearns had total equity amounting to $11.8 billion which supported a balance sheet size of $395 billion. In other words, it was 33 times levered, or put differently it had a ratio of total equity to balance sheet size of 3 percent. But Bear Stearns was not an exception. Many US investment banks and universal banks with large investment banking business also had similar levels of leverage in 2007, and they too came under severe funding stress. Banks with high leverage generally have a significant repo-based funding, whose resilience will depend on perceived safety of the backing collateral assets linked to the size of haircuts. I will discuss the leverage ratio constraint that was introduced to complement the capital ratio measure and the treatment of the liquidity of the repo funding source under the revised Basel rules in the next chapter.

The uncertainty in financial markets remained high after the Bear Stearns bailout. But it was the bankruptcy of Lehman Brothers in September 2008 that set into motion the resolve for a complete overhaul of financial regulation. The underlying factors leading to Lehman failure was not much different from that of Bear Stearns. But because it filed for bankruptcy, the policy lessons from Lehman were more profound and revealed the full complexity of dismantling a large global financial institution.

Considering that Lehman Brothers was a major player providing prime brokerage and derivatives trading services, I will try to focus on the weaknesses as regards how financial contracts were structured that turned out to be a dominant driver of contagion by transmitting liquidity risks to other firms. The policy response to mitigate this risk by mandating the use of central counterparties for derivatives transactions is discussed in a later chapter.

Hedge funds rely on prime brokers for a variety of services: trade execution in cash markets; hedging and risk-taking in derivatives markets; short-term financing of their leveraged positions through collateralised loans; and reconciliation and valuation of their financial positions held in custody accounts. Other institutional investors entering into bilateral derivative transactions with the prime broker will also have to pledge collateral assets to meet initial margin and variation margin payments as a credit risk mitigant. The practice of posting or pledging assets as collateral with the prime broker is called hypothecation. For collateral securities that had been pledged, prime brokers negotiated with clients the rights to rehypothecation in return for cheaper funding or other benefits. Rehypothecation refers to a pledged asset being lent out or re-pledged, which results in the prime brokers' client losing title to the collateral. Instead, the client receives contractual right to the return of fungible collateral, but this claim is unsecured. Not many clients understood the legal implications of their decision to grant rehypothecation rights if the prime broker were to file for bankruptcy.

Across the Atlantic, bankruptcy laws for recovering client assets when a prime broker defaults differ. In the US, the Securities and Exchange Commission rule required client assets to be segregated so that they were not treated as general creditors in the bankruptcy proceedings. But when Lehman's main European broker-dealer based in the UK went into administration, it turned out that client assets were not segregated resulting in their claims falling under the same category as those of general creditors. Hedge funds and other clients also realised that under the UK law, the loss of ownership of their pledged assets from rehypothecation meant that they had to recover these assets as general creditors through insolvency proceedings. The contagion and transmission of liquidity risks resulting in the freezing of credit and derivatives markets in the following weeks can be directly linked to the recognition of risks associated with pledged collateral assets held in margin accounts.

Among others, the failure of Lehman Brothers highlighted problems linked to margining practices on bilateral derivatives contracts, lack of understanding of risks associated with rehypothecation of pledged collateral, importance of enforcing segregation of client assets posted as collateral, and the complexity of unwinding open derivatives trades when a major broker-dealer fails. The bailout of AIG immediately after Lehman bankruptcy also shed more light on poor market practices linked to over-the-counter derivatives trading. AIG had written significant amounts of credit protection through credit default swaps for securitisation products backed by subprime assets. But as a triple-A rated firm, AIG's derivatives counterparties did not require collateral to be posted on its derivatives trades. Yet, built-in rating triggers in these derivatives contracts required AIG to make large collateral payments when its credit rating fell leading to significant liquidity shortages. As this coincided with liquidity shortages facing the securities lending unit of AIG when counterparties returned securities borrowed from AIG and sought cash reimbursement, a government rescue plan had to be put in place to avoid another large financial firms' failure.

The policy response to prevent a repeat of these events was to mandate the central clearing of standardised derivatives products and enforcing margin requirements for all counterparties in the trade. To discourage trading of complex derivatives products that are not eligible for central clearing, revised Basel standards imposed significantly higher capital requirements on these trades. Beyond this, the complexity associated with dismantling a large internationally active financial firm such as Lehman laid the ground work for introducing legislation on effective resolution of financial firms without recourse to taxpayer money.

The failure of Lehman Brothers created turmoil in the US money market fund industry. One fund, the Reserve Primary Fund, could not redeem investors the promised $1 per share, what is referred to in the market jargon as breaking the buck. The fund had substantial holdings of Lehman's short-term debt that led to material losses and had no sponsor backing. As many other money market funds also came under severe stress due to investor withdrawals causing a run on money funds, the US government was forced to intervene.

The policy response to avoid this happening again would have required any of the following actions: prohibiting money market funds to offer $1 net asset value redemptions; mandating funds offering them to be backed by minimum capital requirements; or requiring them to participate in an insurance scheme that will guarantee the $1 net asset value redemptions. The lobbying by money funds was too strong to introduce any of these changes necessary to address the lessons learned. But the US SEC did manage after lengthy debates to change rules that required funds investing in non-government debt to offer floating net asset values as of October 2016, which meant they could break the buck even in normal market conditions.

The contagion from Lehman also spread quickly to Europe. The channel through which this materialised was by triggering an almost complete freeze of interbank funding markets. European banks simply did not trust each other, particularly when lending across borders. The effects of this risk aversion hit Irish banks first which had come to rely on interbank funding to meet the loan demand for residential and commercial mortgages. In June 2008, cross-border interbank funding amounted to about $300 billion, but it fell to $155 billion in March 2009. Again, what the crisis revealed was that interbank funding can disappear in very short time leading to funding crisis, which eventually becomes a solvency crisis. The experience of Irish banks, and subsequently of Spanish banks, was influential in deciding how interbank funding will be treated under the new rules on liquidity regulation in Basel III.

The ad hoc response of authorities in Ireland to extend a blanket guarantee of the liabilities of Irish banks raised many challenges in other euro area countries faced with a weak banking system. This led to other euro area countries being forced to reciprocate by announcing that all bank deposits would be guaranteed for an interim period. This coordination failure was subsequently addressed by the European Commission by mandating every EU country to have identical coverage levels for bank deposit guarantee amounting to €100,000 per depositor.

Perhaps the most important lesson learned for policy from the Irish banking crisis was the need to move away from a narrowly focused microprudential banking regulation to a broader mandate that also includes elements of macroprudential regulation. Let me try to explain what these terms mean. Banking supervisors under the framework of Basel II were simply examining if an individual bank was complying with the requirements in the regulation in terms of capital adequacy and risk management practices. This bank-specific focus is called microprudential regulation. Supervisors were not trained, and also did not have the mandate, to ask banks to take mitigating actions against risks that can materialise from collective actions of other financial market participants. Supervisory process that is designed to assess and respond to the emergence of system-wide risks from collective actions of financial market participants, even if they appear to be uncoordinated, is referred to as macroprudential regulation.

How might macroprudential regulation – if it had existed – been able to temper the risks that were building up in the Irish banking system? To provide some insights, it is important to understand developments in the Irish real estate sector during the period 2003 to 2007. The access to a wider pool of savings in a single currency market and a common monetary policy that was too accommodative for the macroeconomic conditions in Ireland allowed a real estate bubble to develop unhindered. Irish banks gained access to excess savings in other euro area countries through interbank loans. Many UK banks also provided cross-border loans. Rising property values and a huge demand for housing loans led banks to loosen lending standards by offering a significant share of new mortgage loans that had less than 10 percent down payment. That is, the ratio of the bank loan to the value of the property rose to 90 percent or more on close to half of the new loans extended in 2005–07.

If macroprudential regulation had been in place, supervisors could have required all banks to set a maximum loan-to-value ratio limit of 70 percent. Loans that were granted above this limit would have been treated as uncollateralised loan resulting in capital charges to be raised from 35 percent to 100 percent. In addition, supervisors could have increased capital requirements from a minimum 8 percent level to, say, 10 percent level. These actions would have severely constrained the capacity of Irish banks to lend to poorly collateralised housing loans, and as a result, would have applied brakes on the real estate boom. But these tools were not available to supervisors, and the central bank also had no tools to dampen the housing boom by pursuing an independent monetary policy. Post-crisis reforms ensured that supervisors have additional tools to take corrective actions early on that would constrain risk-taking capacity of the entire banking sector.

I will conclude this chapter with the policy lessons drawn from the collapse of the Icelandic banking system in October 2008, which revealed yet another weakness of the pre-crisis financial architecture. The main driver of the banking crisis was the shift away from providing commercial banking services to a local client base until 2002 to offering more foreign currency denominated loans catering to a Europe-wide client base. This resulted in an expansion of bank assets from about 100 percent of GDP in 2002 to about 900 percent of GDP in early 2008.

What is important for policy is the large share of foreign currency assets held and how the Icelandic banks went about funding them. Initially, this asset growth was funded by issuing euro-denominated medium term notes, and subsequently by packaging bank liabilities into collateralised debt obligations and sold to US investors. When the credit markets became non-functional in mid-2007, Icelandic banks began targeting more retail deposits in Europe. Already in October 2006, Icesave was opened in the UK as a branch of Landsbanki, one of the Icelandic banks. Subsequently in May 2008, Icesave as a branch of Landsbanki opened in the Netherlands. In both countries Icesave offered on-line savings accounts to retail customers with interest rates higher than other banks.

A similar strategy was also followed by Kaupthing Bank, another Icelandic bank, for accessing retail deposits from European countries. But in contrast the Icesave, the sourcing of retail funds by offering online savings accounts was done mainly through establishing subsidiaries rather than branches in many countries. This had important legal implications as it shifted responsibility for regulation and deposit guarantees to the host countries where these subsidiaries were established. When saving accounts are offered through branches, the responsibility for deposit guarantee and supervision lies with home authorities where the parent bank is located. What made sourcing of deposits from retail clients in other European countries possible was that Iceland was part of the

European Economic Area by which it had the right to access the single market.

Following the failure of Lehman, the three big banks in Iceland could not roll over the maturing liabilities to fund their large holdings of foreign currency denominated assets. The central bank of Iceland simply did not have the foreign currency reserves needed to provide emergency lending assistance to the banks. The first bank to fail was Landsbanki in early October 2008, soon to be followed by the other two large banks. In normal circumstances, retail savings held in overseas branches would be compensated as per existing rules for deposit insurance coverage in the home country of the parent bank. That amount stood at €20,880 and the deposit insurance scheme in Iceland would have been responsible for compensation payments. The total amount of depositor liabilities at Icesave in the UK and in the Netherlands stood around €4 billion. The insurance scheme or the government of Iceland simply did not have the funds to make such a large foreign currency payment, which prompted the UK and the Netherlands governments to bailout depositors in their respective jurisdictions.

For policy, authorities drew important lessons on the risks to depositor insurance coverage when a bank established operations in a host country as a branch. Indeed, following a dispute over who is liable for the deposit insurance payments, a court ruling found that the government of Iceland was not responsible for the liabilities of the Icelandic deposit insurance scheme given the scale of the banking crisis. But the resolution approach taken by the authorities in Iceland to restore critical operations of Landsbanki also provided useful lessons. The bank was split into a good and bad bank with deposits held in Iceland being transferred to the good bank, and hence were protected. This resolution strategy effectively subordinated the claims of depositors holding accounts in foreign branches versus deposit accounts held in the home country of the bank.

The Icelandic banking crisis provided important lessons on how banks should be structured, what safeguards host authorities need for allowing branches of foreign banks to operate, and what cross-border cooperation and coordination mechanisms are needed among supervisors to safeguard financial stability. The complexity of resolving failed banks with large cross-border operations that are structured both through subsidiary and branch forms gave rise to a new regulatory initiative on key attributes for effective resolution regimes for financial institutions under the leadership of the Financial Stability Board.

CHAPTER NINE

REDESIGNING BASEL

The post-mortem of the crisis I presented in earlier chapters highlighted areas where existing financial regulation had a number of weaknesses. Regulation was also designed to monitor risks that might build up in individual financial institutions' balance sheet rather than in the financial system as a whole. A redesigned Basel III provided a framework under which both bank-specific and system-wide risks can be adequately monitored and corrective actions can be taken.

My plan for this chapter is to make a link between weaknesses in banking regulation that allowed market participants to take excessive risks contributing to the crisis, and how changed rules under Basel III goes about fixing them. But it is not meant to be comprehensive of all rule changes that were introduced. For benefit of readers, I will highlight some debates and discussions that took place while these rules were being drafted. In terms of structure, I will first present the changes in capital regulation including macroprudential regulation, then follow it up with the new rules on liquidity regulation, and finally discuss the minimum leverage ratio as complementary measure to the minimum capital ratio.

Let me begin with reforms to raise the quality of the capital base as certain capital instruments permitted under Basel II turned out to be not capable of absorbing losses under liquidation. A key element of the revised standards is the emphasis on common equity for meeting minimum regulatory capital requirements. Under Basel III, regulatory capital is divided into Tier 1 capital referred to as going-concern capital, and Tier 2 capital referred to as gone-concern capital. Tier 1 capital is then divided into two categories – the common equity Tier 1 (CET1) and additional Tier 1 (AT1) capital.

CET1 capital typically includes common shares issued by the bank, retained earnings and other disclosed reserves. Goodwill and other intangibles as well as deferred tax assets that rely on future profitability of the bank are to be deducted from CET1 capital because they have no loss-absorbing capacity under liquidation. AT1 capital includes preferred shares and other instruments that have loss-absorbing capacity. Because of the emphasis on CET1 capital under Basel III for meeting capital requirements, AT1 capital instruments issued by banks are often hybrid capital instruments that turn out to be either common shares or junior subordinated debt in different states of the world. That is, they are issued as convertible instruments and the conversion to common shares happen when the bank fails to meet the minimum capital requirements through CET1 capital instruments. One example is a hybrid instrument called contingent convertible or CoCo bonds issued by the bank that has gained some popularity as an AT1 capital instrument.

The category of instruments to be included under Tier 2 capital did not change from those that were permitted under Basel II. For example, these include subordinated debt, undisclosed reserves, asset revaluation reserves and general loan loss provisions.

Let me make a remark here on the calculation of general loss provisions that came under much scrutiny during the crisis. This was linked to the delayed recognition of loan losses in financial accounts that allowed profits to be reported even when senior management of banks recognised that large losses may occur with high probability. That is because financial accounting standards required loan loss provisions to be set aside only when there was objective evidence to the occurrence of these losses. In contrast to this, the prudential accounting practices for loan loss provisioning, that is the one set by bank supervisors under Basel II and Basel III, was based on the expected loss model that is meant to be forward-looking. Following persistent efforts by the Financial Stability Board, the accounting standards bodies (IASB and FASB) agreed to move financial reporting for loan loss provisioning from an impairment-based model to an expected loss-based model to address an important pre-crisis short-coming of inflating profits ahead of large balance sheet losses to be incurred. The new rules will take effect in January 2018.

The revised Basel III standards set the minimum total capital requirement as a share of risk-weighted assets to be the same as under Basel II, that is at 8 percent. But the requirements for high quality capital were raised by setting CET1 capital ratio to be at least 4.5 percent and Tier 1 capital ratio to be at least 6 percent. The remaining 2 percent could be met by Tier 2 capital instruments or higher quality capital. Beyond the minimum capital requirements, additional capital requirements are imposed under macroprudential regulatory rules which I will discuss later in this chapter.

A major flaw of the Basel II standards was the underestimation of the risks of some exposures based on the wrong expectation that banks will exercise prudence when taking on those risks. This led to the assignment of risk weights for those exposures that were not commensurate with the potential losses that could materialise in adverse states of the world. Increasing the risk weights on certain exposures held on the asset side of the balance sheet raises the amount of risk-weighted assets, and consequently lowers the capital ratio for a given amount of Tier 1 capital held. Drawing lessons from the crisis, Basel III risk weights were raised for a number of exposures that are described below.

The financial crisis has been attributed by many to the poor underwriting practices in the real estate market. This needed to be fixed. The Basel II rules oversimplified the risk weight to be applied to residential mortgage exposures by stipulating that if it is backed by mortgage collateral, then the applicable risk weight is 35 percent. It provided no incentive to prudent lenders who lent only 70 percent of the mortgage value as opposed to another lender giving 90 percent of the value of the property as loan. In the first case, the loan-to-value (LTV) ratio would be 70 percent, whereas in the latter case it would be 90 percent. To alter incentives and encourage prudent lending standards to develop, the revised Basel III risk weights for residential mortgage lending backed by collateral become progressively higher as the LTV ratio rises. For example, for LTV ratios between 60 and 80 percent, risk weight is set to 35 percent; for LTV ratios between 80 and 90 percent, the risk weight is 45 percent; and for 90 to 100 percent LTV ratios, the risk weight becomes 55 percent.

The risk weights under Basel III also take into consideration whether the residential property being acquired falls under the category of owner-occupied or buy-to-let. In the latter case, the cash flows from rental income determine the repayments on the mortgage loan. Historically, as well as during the crisis, such mortgage loans have resulted in more defaults as they are often made in periods of overheated property market. For such loans the risk weights have been set to 90 percent when LTV ratios are between 60 and 80 percent, and beyond 80 percent LTV ratios the risk weight assigned is 120 percent. Finally, when the loan taken is in a different currency from the currency of borrower's main source of income, Basel III includes an add-on of 50 percent risk weight to those without currency mismatch. This applies to both owner-occupied and buy-to-let mortgage loans.

The risk weights for collateralised commercial mortgage lending have also been linked to the LTV ratio of the loan, and when LTV ratio is higher than 80 percent, the risk weight has been set to 130 percent. This is higher than the 100 percent risk weight under Basel II without regard to underwriting standards. Basel III rules now send a clear signal to banks making mortgage loans that underwriting standards will be closely monitored, and a stick and carrot rule will be used to promote improved lending standards.

Another area where policy intervention was needed is in the treatment of off-balance sheet exposures. These arise when a bank extends a credit commitment to a retail or non-retail counterparty but remains undrawn at the time of reporting capital requirements. Under Basel II, generous discounts were given by allowing banks to use a credit conversion factor (CCF). In the extreme case, when the credit commitments were structured to be unconditionally cancellable by the banks, the CCF was set to zero, meaning that the undrawn credit was discounted 100 percent from capital charges. In cases where they were structured to be available for less than one year, large discounts were available relative to granting them for more than one year. For example, a CCF of 50 percent for commitments greater than one year would be reduced to 20 percent if banks reported that the commitment was for less than one year. Banks had considerable scope for gaming the rules in their favour.

Indeed in the run-up to the crisis, off-balance sheet exposures arising from liquidity and credit commitments extended to SIVs sponsored by banks did not attract meaningful capital charges. Yet, the availability of these lines of credit and liquidity from sponsoring banks were taken into consideration by rating agencies in justifying a higher credit rating to the counterparty receiving them without regard to whether they were unconditionally cancellable. Rating agencies' opinion was confirmed when banks extended credit support when those vehicles came under distress even though the commitments were structured to be unconditionally cancellable. In cases where the commitments were actually withdrawn, it accelerated the bankruptcy of the counterparty and amplified financial instability.

Important changes were made in Basel III rules to reflect the true risks that banks held when entering into credit commitments based on lessons learned from the financial crisis, and to ensure that banks set aside adequate capital for those risks. A first change was to disregard the maturity of the credit commitment when determining the CCF for the undrawn line of credit. In particular, if a credit commitment for more than one year has a CCF of 50 percent, then it will remain the same even if the commitment period has been reduced to six months or one month under the revised rules.

The proposed changes to the treatment of unconditionally cancellable commitments, however, have been vehemently opposed by the industry. These commitments received full capital relief as Basel II allowed CCF to be set to zero in such cases. Anyone analysing the pre-crisis regulatory rules would flag this one as being poorly designed. Under Basel III rules, retail unconditionally cancellable commitments have been proposed to receive a CCF value between 10 to 20 percent. All other non-retail commitments structured to be unconditionally cancellable are to be treated as general commitments. As a result, they will receive a CCF value between 50 and 75 percent. Final rule making was still pending as of end-2016.

Risk weights for securitisation exposures in Basel II came under much criticism as they did not adequately capture the underlying risks. Responding to this criticism, the revisions to risk weights applicable to securitisation exposures have been very comprehensive. But it also makes a simple exposition of these changes difficult to capture in a non-technical language. I will therefore use the risk weights using the external ratings-based approach under Basel III to provide insights on the changes in capital requirements.

A key change to the risk charge determination for securitisation exposures is to categorise securitisations as being either simple, transparent and comparable (STC) or falling outside this category. Additionally, risk weights have been made sensitive to the maturity of the securitisation exposure as well as to the level of subordination that a given securitised tranche has. To meet the STC criteria, the assets underlying the securitisation should be credit claims or receivables that are homogenous, and the transaction structure should not be complex. The homogeneity criterion is likely to be met, if for example, the asset type, the jurisdiction where the claims on assets are to be met, and the currency denomination of the assets are all the same. The STC criteria would be met for simple securitisations of credit card receivables, student loans, or residential mortgage assets originated in a particular country. A comparison of the risk weights for securitisation assets under Basel II and the revised Basel III standards are shown in Box 4. The new standards will come into force in January 2018.

Box 4: Risk weights under IRB approach for securitised assets						
	Basel II		Basel III (1 year tranche maturity)			
			STC compliant		All others	
Credit rating	Senior	Non-senior	Senior	Non-senior	Senior	Non-senior
AAA	7%	8%	10%	15%	15%	15%
AA	12%	15%	15%	15%	25%	30%
A	12%	20%	30%	60%	50%	80%
BBB	60%	75%	55%	180%	90%	220%

The revised rules under Basel III have also been made stricter in determining whether a bank that sells assets through a securitisation transaction will receive capital relief or not. In circumstances where a bank provides support to the securitisation transaction through credit risk mitigants or other means, capital relief will not be granted. Capital charges for resecuritisation exposures have also been raised substantially in Basel III with the minimum risk weight set to 100 percent.

While analysing the factors that increased the severity of the crisis, I highlighted the procyclical effects of leverage in the financial system created through repo and other securities financing transactions (SFT). Mitigating the risks to financial stability from these transactions by establishing minimum standards on haircuts and eligible collateral assets has been another important reform agenda.

Let me begin with a definition of SFT. Banks and broker-dealers lend securities to counterparties which promote market liquidity and facilitate trade execution. Against the securities lent, either cash or other securities are received as collateral to mitigate counterparty risk. When cash is received as collateral, the transaction goes by the name repo. But when a security is received as collateral, the transaction goes by the name securities lending. Prime brokers use securities lending programmes to help them meet customer buy orders, finance short sales or engage in collateral upgrade transactions, that is lend lower quality securities and receive higher quality collateral securities such as government bonds.

A major weakness in Basel II was that banks were given the freedom to set the haircut on these collateralised transactions using past one year of market data, which were subject to sudden and large increases in times of market stress. The policy intervention under the reform agenda has been very comprehensive. In a nutshell they include the following: preclude resecuritisation assets to be used as collateral; disallow banks' own estimates of haircuts on collateral assets; use stressed market conditions to come up with supervisory haircuts; set higher supervisory haircuts for securitised assets in relation to those for corporate securities of comparable credit ratings; and to establish haircut floors taking into account both legs of a SFT. I will elaborate on some of these to illustrate how the proposed changes will alter market discipline and reduce procyclicality.

Consider a SFT where a bank lends $102 worth of 2-year corporate bond to a client and receives $105 worth of 2-year maturity securitised asset as collateral with both securities rated AA. Under Basel III, the supervisory haircut for the corporate bond will be 3 percent and for the securitised asset it will be 8 percent. The bank will have to compute the net exposure for this SFT to ascertain if this transaction requires capital to be set aside. For this trade, the net exposure will be computed using the following formula:

Net exposure = maximum [0; 102x(1+0.03) − 105x(1-0.08)]

The net exposure turns out to be $8.46, which under the 8 percent minimum capital requirement standard and a 100 percent risk weight assumption for the counterparty will result in a capital charge of 68 cents in the revised Basel III standards. The earlier standards under Basel II allowed banks to self-determine appropriate haircuts subject to supervisory approval. If the bank had set the applicable haircuts to 3 percent for both securities, the net exposure would amount to $3.46 and the capital charge will be only 26 cents. If market conditions change and the bank assesses that the haircut on the securitised asset has to increase to 8 percent, the bank will request an additional $5 worth of the same collateral asset to keep its capital charges the same following this assessment. This will force the client to deleverage if they cannot meet the margin call. If similar actions are also taken by other banks, it will set in motion a powerful procyclical deleveraging mechanism. By setting more conservative supervisory haircuts applicable through the business cycle, the extent of procyclical dynamics stemming from haircut setting and margining practices will be dampened.

Market disciple has been enforced in Basel III for SFT by setting haircut floors for these transactions that fall under the category of non-centrally cleared. The standards text in Basel III assigns a haircut floor of 1.5 percent for the corporate bond and 4 percent for the securitised asset in question. Skipping the details, the haircut floor for this SFT involving a corporate bond and a securitised asset turns out to be 2.46 percent. Because $105 of the collateral received is backing $102 of the corporate bond lent, the effective haircut for the bank financing this transaction is 2.94 percent (ratio of 105 over 102 minus 1). As this is above the haircut floor, no additional capital charges apply. On the other hand, had the bank only taken $104.5 worth of securitised assets as collateral, the effective haircut with which the bank has entered into this SFT will turn out to be 2.45 percent. Because this value is lower than the supervisory haircut floor, the transaction will be treated as uncollateralised lending so that the bank will have to treat the corporate bond lent as a full exposure to the client. This will require the bank to set aside $8.16 for capital charges, which will discipline banks to demand adequate collateral to back SFT.

Another area of reform where international negotiations are still facing some challenges is in having a capital floor framework when banks use internal model to compute risk-weighted assets. The motivation behind the capital floor framework is to prevent undue optimism in bank's internal risk modelling practices by constraining permissible variations in model-derived risk weights for exposures. This is to be achieved by setting a floor on the risk weight for a given exposure using internal models as a percent of the risk weight of the same exposure under the standardised approach.

The background for the capital floor is that when the Basel Committee conducted quantitative impact study for the proposed regulatory changes for a representative portfolio, the risk-weighted assets showed large variations across banks participating in the study. Without stating the obvious, it was clear that in some jurisdictions supervisors were far more lenient in allowing large banks to overestimate their capital ratios by employing their internal models. Creating a level playing field across jurisdictions required reaching an international agreement on a capital floor for risk weights in order to enforce greater consistency of internal risk model estimates.

German authorities have stalled progress in this important reform supported by Sweden and France. The contention has been that in Germany and Sweden mortgages comprise large share of bank loans and these are safer than those in other countries. But Sweden went through a major banking crisis triggered by poor quality mortgage loans in the early 1990s, and if history is any guide, Swedish mortgage loans cannot be safer than those in other countries. In Germany, mortgage loans of the two largest banks are only about 10 percent of total assets, whereas for some large US banks it is higher. The source of underestimation of risk is more likely to be those related to loans for small and medium-sized corporates.

Capital requirements for market risk have also been revised under Basel III beyond those introduced immediately after the crisis. That initial revision took into account volatility in stressed market conditions to estimate the capital charges. A more fundamental change to take effect in 2019 will be a move away from the value-at-risk measure to determine capital requirements for the trading book exposures. In its place, another measure called the expected shortfall will be introduced for computing capital requirements. Further, risk charges for capturing default risk of credit and equity exposures in the trading book will also be introduced. This goes under the name credit value adjustment (CVA) charge.

The motivation to use expected shortfall for market risk is that it provides a better estimate of the trading book losses when it exceeds a certain threshold, such as at a 99 percent confidence level. If, for instance, there are two outcomes for the losses that exceed this confidence level, one of $10 and another of $100. The value-at-risk measure will report the capital required to withstand losses at 99 percent confidence level as $10. The expected shortfall, on the other hand, will take the average of the two losses, which is $55, and report this as the expected shortfall at the 99 percent confidence level. That is, expected shortfall is more conservative and provides a better estimate of the so-called tail risks embedded in trading book portfolios. But it also has a useful mathematical property that is important for the banking business. Specifically, if a bank were to combine the trading books of its London and Frankfurt subsidiaries to compute an aggregate expected shortfall, this would be lower than if the expected shortfalls for the two units were computed independently and summed up. That is, expected shortfall recognises better the diversification benefits in a portfolio. The value at risk measure does not share this property.

What I have described so far refers to changes to microprudential regulation where bank-specific risks are meant to be addressed by strengthened capital regulation. Yet, system-wide risks can build-up during the expansion phase of the business cycle even if bank-specific risks appear not to be worrisome. This is because banking business is inherently procyclical where the credit supply tends to ebb and flow as the business cycle conditions change, and so does system-wide risks. The Basel Committee recognised that reducing the effects of adverse spillover to the real economy through this ebb and flow of system-wide risks in response to changes in business conditions requires macroprudential regulation. This under Basel III is delivered through requirements to hold a capital conservation buffer and a countercyclical capital buffer. Let me now elaborate on them.

The Basel standards set minimum capital requirements for banks. By stating explicitly that it is minimum, regulators expected that banks will be prudent and hold more capital to take them through a rainy day. Unfortunately, banks interpreted minimum to imply target capital requirements, and when capital ratios exceeded this level they made generous dividend distributions to shareholders. This is like consuming your entire harvest half way through the winter with the hope that this years' winter will be mild and short. This practice was also not questioned by microprudential regulators who assumed that their task was to provide certification of pass when banks met their minimum capital ratio requirements.

Because encouraging banks to hold more capital than their minimum requirements under Basel II failed miserably, the new Basel III standards has changed language and is mandating banks to hold additional capital. This shift in language was needed as the banking industry faced what economists refer to as a collective action problem. Specifically, banks used generous dividend distributions and employee bonus payments as a signalling device to markets that they remained profitable even if their individual financial condition and the outlook for the sector were deteriorating. No bank wanted to be the first to report bad news. A backward-looking financial accounting standards based on an incurred loss model also helped banks to pursue this strategy and reward shareholders to the detriment of creditor interests.

The capital conservation buffer can be thought of as one of the tools being employed by regulators to address the collective action problem. It is meant to help banks be more resilient when the economy enters into a downturn with strong capital positions so that the banking sector is a source of strength rather than an amplifier of risks to the financial system and the real economy. Towards this goal, banks are expected to build a capital conservation buffer comprising of common equity Tier 1 instruments during normal times constituting up to 2.5 percent of the risk-weighted assets. The capital conservation buffer can be compared to that of a water reservoir where stored water is released during the dry season and refilled during the rainy season by pursuing prudent water management strategies.

The specific tools employed by regulators to build the capital conservation buffer is to require banks to reduce dividend payments, share-buybacks and bonus payments in normal times until the capital buffer has 2.5 percent of risk-weighted assets in the form of CET1 instruments. Alternatively, banks could also raise this capital directly from shareholders. In situations where the buffer does not meet the target level, specific guidance is given in Basel III as regards what restrictions apply to distributions as a function of the shortfall from the target level. Dividend payments, share-buybacks and bonus payments fall under the category of distributions.

The views as to whether the capital conservation buffer should fall under micro or macroprudential regulation differ even among regulators. One reason for this is that Basel III provides very clear guidance on regulatory interventions needed to ensure that banks build this capital buffer. For example, if the capital conservation buffer has less than 0.625 percent of risk-weighted assets, no capital distributions are permitted. Prescriptive rules are often considered to be the responsibility of microprudential regulators. But the debate is also linked to which authority will be responsible for oversight and banks' compliance with these rules. More importantly, if situations demand that this buffer can be drawn down by the banking system, which authority should be responsible for that decision?

The ECB under the single supervisory mechanism retains responsibility for the capital conservation buffer with the implication that it sees this as the responsibility of microprudential regulators. Yet, the Basel Committee's deliberations focused on the motivation for introducing the capital conservation buffer, which it argues is for reducing the procyclicality of the financial system as well as for the banking system in the aggregate to withstand unexpected shocks without being forced to sell assets or raise capital in difficult market conditions to meet minimum capital requirements. That has a macroprudential focus by targeting banking system problems.

Let me now turn to the countercyclical capital buffer and the motivation for its introduction. Many of the banking system problems, not just during the recent financial crisis, are often preceded by excessive credit growth during the expansion phase of the financial cycle. Should regulatory authorities dampen such credit cycles as it gathers pace, and if so, what tools are best suited to restrain them? Much time was spent debating this question. A natural candidate would be to raise short-term interest rates set by the central bank under its monetary policy framework. Yet, being a blunt tool, it affects borrowing costs for every sector of the economy, some of which may not be contributing to excessive credit growth. Banks also find innovative ways to shift the rising interest rate burden to the private sector, particularly home owners with little financial literacy, and continue to fuel the credit growth. The financial crisis provided many lessons on this.

International policy making converged on employing a countercyclical capital buffer for banks as it was assessed to provide a good trade-off to dampen excessive credit growth without having adverse effects on the real economy. At the same time, the countercyclical buffer was meant to achieve the broader macroprudential goal of protecting the banking sector during times of excessive aggregate credit growth. The maximum size of the buffer is set at 2.5 percent of the risk-weighted assets with the expectation that in normal times the buffer will be set to zero. The buffer should comprise CET1 instruments, which is capital of highest quality that can absorb losses.

The language used in Basel III is that the activation of the countercyclical buffer is discretionary and has to be communicated well in advance by regulators – typically several quarters. Because of the discretionary nature of the activation and the need to have a supervisory assessment that justifies its activation, the Basel III standards require a separate macroprudential authority to be responsible for the process. Indeed, the same macroprudential authority is also tasked to have oversight and responsibility for safeguarding the stability of the financial system.

When a macroprudential authority raises the countercyclical capital buffer requirements above zero to credit exposures within its jurisdiction, foreign banks having exposure to this jurisdiction are required to comply. Some countries have implemented rules allowing them to alter sectoral capital requirements in a countercyclical manner. An example is to increase risk weights above the levels applicable in normal times for mortgage loans if excessive mortgage lending is driving up house prices. Any additional capital charges resulting from activation of the countercyclical buffer has to be well-articulated and communicated transparently to the general public.

Beyond these buffers, namely the capital conservation and countercyclical ones, there is an additional buffer for systemically large financial institutions that could go up to 5 percent of risk-weighted assets. But the main message coming from regulators is that the 4 percent Tier 1 capital ratio under Basel II is far too low to build a resilient global financial system. The capital requirements based on the crisis experience have been raised almost 3 fold in normal times. All the capital buffers will be fully operational as of January 2019.

Will the higher capital requirements for bank lending constrain economic growth? This became the contentious question during discussions between banks and the regulatory authorities. Banks argued that the increased capital charges will reduce global growth by up to 0.5 percentage points per year over the implementation period. In addition, the higher capital charges will result in reduced bank lending and increase bank interest spreads to the real economy.

The view of the authorities was that higher interest spreads are not a bad thing as risk spreads were too compressed during the run up to the crisis that partly contributed to the excess credit growth. Results based on models routinely used by central banks for their monetary policy frameworks did not show the same level of reduction in economic growth as claimed by banks. Moreover, much of the loss in economic output happens when a banking crisis occurs, and a deep crisis tends to depress GDP growth over the longer term. By reducing the frequency and severity of banking crisis by mandating banks to hold more capital, central banks were of the view that a small reduction in annual growth is well worth the price to pay to avoid deep and protracted recessions stemming from an under-capitalised banking system.

What I have discussed so far are reforms to strengthen capital requirements associated with the asset side of the bank balance sheet. The Basel II standards focused explicitly on the asset side with the view that threats to solvency arise from poor loan quality or loans linked to risky projects that may have to be written off. But the crisis experience, and in particular the threats to solvency of Northern Rock, did not arise only from poor asset quality. Rather, the inability to issue debt to fund the assets had an important role to play, and it demonstrated the close links between funding liquidity risk and risk of insolvency. This policy lesson led regulators to recognise that how banks go about funding their liabilities may also precipitate financial crisis, and regulation should take a more holistic view of bank balance sheets that include both the asset and liability sides.

The policy response was to introduce new regulation mandating banks to take an integrated view of how they go about issuing liabilities to fund their assets. This led to two new standards on liquidity management for banks referred to as the liquidity coverage ratio (LCR) and the net stable funding ratio (NSFR) to promote a more resilient banking system. Banks have to be fully compliant with NSFR from January 2018 onwards, and on LCR a transitional arrangement allows for 80 percent compliance with the rules as of 2017, which is to be raised to full compliance level in January 2019.

Let me now provide some details on the LCR and its motivation. First, some terminology is needed to understand the liquidity regulation. One is the notion of high quality liquid assets (HQLA), which in turn is broken down into level 1, level 2A and level 2B categories. Another is the concept of cash outflows, which establishes the resilience of a given liability that the bank has issued. A third one is cash inflows, which provides an estimate of the funds that will be available from counterparties on outstanding transactions as well as from maturing secured lending transactions.

In a nutshell, the LCR makes banks recognise the quality and liquidity of assets it holds when considering how those assets should be funded to reduce the risk that it may be faced with liquidity shortages in the short-term. Towards this goal, banks have to compute the stock of HQLA in stressed market conditions as a share of the net cash outflows (cash outflows minus cash inflows) over the next 30 calendar days. The minimum standards for LCR compliance require that this ratio exceeds 100 percent.

The rules in liquidity regulation provide explicit guidance on how different assets need to be weighted when computing the stock of HQLA. For example, level 1 category assets carry a 100 percent weight. That is, all these assets count towards stock of HQLA without discounting. Level 2A assets are to be weighted by 85 percent and level 2B by 75 or 50 percent. The specific details of these different asset categories and their weights are not important. What I would like to emphasise here though is that all assets that are encumbered, such as those backing collateralised funding transactions or covered bonds which the bank has issued, do not count towards the stock of HQLA.

Recall that when I discussed the Northern Rock case, I mentioned that the asset encumbrance created by their excessive reliance on secured funding had implicitly lowered potential recovery values for unsecured creditors in bankruptcy that led to loss of this funding source. When a bank holds a covered bond or a mortgage-backed security as an asset, it gets favourable treatment as a level 2A or 2B asset in determining the stock of HQLA. However, if a bank issues secured liabilities resulting in the encumbrance of assets that back these claims, those assets cannot be counted anymore towards the stock of HQLA. This is an important element of the policy reform delivered through liquidity regulation based on lessons learned from the crisis.

To determine cash outflows, which focus on the structure and type of liabilities, funding liabilities that are less resilient receive a higher weighting. Interbank deposits and secured funding backed by assets that do not fall under level 1 or 2 categories are assumed to be least resilient and therefore receive a 100 percent weight. That is, all of these liabilities will be counted towards cash outflows. Retail deposits and other deposits covered by deposit insurance schemes are assumed to be resilient and receive close to zero percent weighting.

The cash inflows over the 30 calendar day period are assessed based on whether the counterparty can be considered safe to honour the contractual payment. But a credit or a liquidity facility provided by another bank is to be disregarded as a source of cash inflow. This is done to eliminate interdependence among banks when it comes to liquidity insurance policies. The net cash outflows are then computed as cash outflows minus cash inflows. The stock of HQLA divided by net cash outflows has to be greater than one to meet the minimum standards for LCR.

Whereas the LCR intends to address liquidity risks banks face in the short-term, Basel Committees' view has been that it needs to be complemented by standards that also promote resilient bank funding structures that take a long term perspective. To achieve this goal, the second liquidity standard called the NSFR limits banks' overreliance on short-term wholesale funding and encourages a better assessment of funding risks stemming from all on- and off-balance sheet exposures. The NSFR is defined as the amount of available stable funding (ASF) divided by the amount of required stable funding (RSF), and this ratio when expressed in percent should exceed 100 to meet the minimum standard.

Similar to the LCR calculation, the amount of ASF is calculated by first assigning the carrying value of a bank's capital and liabilities to one of five risk weighting categories, and then multiplying these amounts by the corresponding ASF factor to compute the total weighted sum. The required stable funding, which appears in the denominator of the NSFR, focuses on the asset side of the balance sheet to compute the amount of RSF based on assigned RSF factors for different category of assets according to their residual maturity or liquidity value. The RSF factors vary from 0 to 100 percent, and assets that have been encumbered, which happen if they back collateralised funding liabilities, receive a 100 percent RSF factor. This increases the amount of RSF and in turn lowers the NSFR ratio.

To provide some intuition behind the NSFR standard, let me take a close proxy of the Northern Rock balance sheet example as of end-2006. Out of $100 billion in assets, $50 billion of assets are encumbered as they back collateralised funding instruments. These assets receive 100 percent RSF factor. Let us assume $45 billion are unencumbered residential mortgage loans with loan-to-value ratio 70 percent so that a RSF factor of 65 percent will be assigned. Remaining $5 billion can be assumed to be in cash and central bank reserves so that it receives zero percent RSF factor. The amount of RSF for this asset exposure will be $79.25 billion. On the liability side, let us assume the composition to be $5 billion equity, $25 billion retail deposits, $25 billion short-term wholesale funding (less than 6 months), $20 billion medium-term wholesale funding (6 months to 1 year), and $25 long-term (more than one year) wholesale funding. The assigned ASF factors for these liabilities will result in the ASF amount to be $63.75 billion. Under this balance sheet structure, the proxy Northern Rock bank would not meet the NSFR minimum standard.

The interesting point to note here is that despite having good quality mortgage assets, the asset encumbrance created by seeking collateralised and covered bond funding leads to the NSFR requirement not being met. If the bank had only issued uncollateralised wholesale debt with an identical maturity structure, the NSFR requirement would be met because the amount of RSF in this case would be only $61.75 billion. The NSFR targets both excessive maturity mismatches as well as excessive asset encumbrance. Many debates on NSFR miss the latter point and its importance in the context of bank resolution. High levels of asset encumbrance create challenges for bank resolution. When more assets in bank balance sheets are encumbered, it lowers recovery value not only for deposit insurance schemes but also for unsecured creditors. For this reason, in stressed markets increased

encumbrance of balance sheets can create a wholesale funding run.
The NSFR has been designed to mitigate this risk besides the risk of
excessive maturity transformation.

The usefulness of NSFR as a microprudential liquidity
regulation standard has been questioned in a number of forums and
by the industry. Reaching consensus even among the global
regulatory community took time. This is because banks' role in the
economy is considered to be the provision of liquidity and maturity
transformation. That is, demand deposits collected from retail
customers who seek safety and liquidity features is transformed by
banks into illiquid, riskier and longer term loans to entrepreneurs,
households and non-financial corporates by managing the risks
related to these activities. The NSFR standard, in the view of some,
was seen as counter-intuitive to the role of banks.

Yet, the traditional banking system, which was built on
collecting redeemable deposits from retail customers and then
lending them to entrepreneurs after adding a risk spread, is being
pursued only by smaller regional banks. The NSFR standard
promotes such a banking system and allows banks to play the role
of maturity and liquidity transformers. What the NSFR penalises is a
different banking model that developed in the pre-crisis period.
That is to issue short-term debt often backed by collateral that was
illiquid to reduce funding costs without taking adequate liquidity
insurance policies.

Let us for a moment focus on the proxy Northern Rock
balance sheet example I mentioned above. Why is the bank issuing
long-term covered bonds and other secured funding liabilities
instead of issuing unsecured wholesale liabilities? The motivation is
simple – it helps the bank lower its cost of funding by issuing
secured liabilities. Unsecured liabilities of identical maturities require
higher interest spreads to attract investors. The remedy is to issue
short-term liabilities at lower spreads, typically 90 days or less,
targeting money fund institutional investors. When funding liquidity
is abundant, the bank generates more profits due to lower funding
cost, and can distribute more dividends to shareholders and reward
bank management generously. When the tide turns, it shifts the
bailout costs to unsecured creditors (and to taxpayers in pre-crisis

period). The NSFR forces banks to internalise these costs in their funding structures.

One other fundamental reform under Basel III has been the introduction of a minimum leverage ratio of 3 percent that will come into force in January 2018. For global systemically important banks (GSIBs), the minimum ratio is intended to be higher. Banks have been obliged to make public disclosure of this ratio already as of January 2015. The leverage ratio is intended to be a complementary measure to capital ratio to provide additional safeguards against model risk that can arise when calculating risk-weighted assets. The leverage ratio is defined as the ratio of Tier 1 capital to an exposure measure that captures the size of the balance sheet and is to be met under the Pillar 1 requirement for banks.

Most of the complexity regarding the computation of the leverage ratio lies in how the derivatives exposures, netting arrangements, initial margins received and securities financing transactions are to be treated to compute the exposure measure that is the denominator of the leverage ratio calculation. Securities financing transactions are accounted for in gross amount without recognising any netting from collateral received. This has the benefit of avoiding inconsistencies from netting which may arise across different accounting regimes. As a general rule, financial collateral received, credit guarantees or credit mitigation techniques are not permitted to be used for reducing the exposure measure. For off-balance sheet exposures, the same credit conversion factor that is applicable under capital regulation to the specific exposure is to be used as the weighting factor to compute the amount of contribution to the exposure measure.

The leverage ratios that banks have been publishing since 2015 suggest that most banks have built up capital and have been able to meet the 3 percent minimum leverage ratio standard. Yet, if GSIBs are required to hold a higher minimum leverage ratio, some banks in Europe will have to raise more capital. In Switzerland, the two large Swiss banks have been required by their regulators to comply with higher leverage ratio standard set at 5 percent.

Readers will recognise the comprehensiveness of the reform package under Basel III to build a resilient financial system. It has taken almost 9 years after the Lehman failure to finalise the standards. Changing banking regulatory rules is a lengthy process requiring impact assessment studies to be conducted, holding consultations with various stakeholders and reaching international consensus to ensure consistency of implementation across jurisdictions. This is one of the reasons why I mentioned in an earlier chapter that even if certain unsustainable trends of bank risk-taking behaviour was spotted, regulatory tools simply did not exist to mitigate the risks as banks played by the rule book. That rule book has now been changed after a difficult international negotiation process taking 9 years. But it has been faster than achieving consensus on climate change negotiations.

CHAPTER TEN

CENTRAL COUNTERPARTY

Trading strategies routinely employed by market participants to take risk or reduce risk are often implemented through derivatives positions. Usually a prime broker or a universal bank often becomes the counterparty to the trade, and such transactions are referred to as over-the-counter (OTC) derivatives. The Lehman Brothers bankruptcy showed that outstanding derivative trades of clients with a defaulted prime broker is a source of systemic risk. Reducing risk in OTC derivatives markets has been another important reform agenda.

Let me begin with an illustrative OTC derivatives transaction to motivate the need for reforms. Consider a non-financial corporate that has issued $10 million worth of a 5-year maturity bond paying a fixed annual interest rate of 3 percent. Suppose a year after issuing the bond the corporate treasurer is of the view that medium-term interest rates are likely to fall to 2.5 percent over the next six months. To benefit from the fall in interest rates when holding a fixed rate bond liability, the corporate treasurer can convert the fixed interest rate liability into a floating rate liability by entering into a 4-year maturity interest rate swap with its commercial bank for a notional amount of $10 million. In this trade, which falls under the category of OTC derivatives trade, the corporate will pay the bank a 3-month floating rate on $10 million notional that will be reset every quarter based on prevailing short-term 3-month interbank rates. In its place, the corporate will receive from the commercial bank a fixed rate coupon that was negotiated on the date of the trade.

Suppose the commercial bank does not have another outstanding position against which this trade can be hedged. In this case, the bank will enter into an offsetting trade with a large universal bank in which it receives the fixed rate and pays the floating rate coupon on a $10 million notional interest rate swap. The two trades of the commercial bank cancel each other out so that there is no net interest rate exposure. Let us assume that after 4 months the interest rates fall to 2.5 percent and the corporate treasurer is glad to unwind his hedging interest rate swap transaction. To do this the treasurer will simply enter into another interest rate swap transaction. Because non-standard swaps are expensive (those like maturing in 3 years and 8 months), the treasurer will enter into another 4-year maturity swap to receive floating interest rate and pay fixed interest rate. This is the reverse of the previous trade the treasurer executed to hedge against a fall in interest rates. Following this trade, the commercial bank may also do a reverse trade with the universal bank to mitigate its risk exposure.

The concerns of regulators from a financial stability point of view stem from the four outstanding OTC derivatives trades held by the commercial bank. The two interest rate swaps the commercial bank has with the non-financial corporate are not closed, and the cash flows also do not match exactly. Both transactions will cease to exist only in 4 years although the first one will expire a few months earlier than this. The commercial bank also has two interest rate swap trades outstanding with the universal bank. Altogether, the notional amount of interest rate swap contracts outstanding from this hedging transaction initiated by the corporate is $40 million (four trades each worth $10 million notional amount). However, the net exposure of the commercial bank with the corporate and the universal bank is much lower under the condition that it has bilateral netting agreements with the two counterparties.

To provide a nuance to this trade, let us assume that the commercial bank decides to do the second leg of the trade to unwind its interest rate risk with a different universal bank, and let us call it the foreign bank. In this case the notional outstanding amount of interest rate swaps will still be $40 million but the net exposures will be significantly higher as both the universal bank and the foreign bank have unhedged interest rate risks against the commercial bank.

To provide some statistics, as of June 2016 the outstanding notional amount of all derivatives contracts is about $545 trillion. Of this, interest rate swaps amount to $325 trillion and foreign exchange (FX) derivatives about $85 trillion. But the gross replacement value of all derivatives contracts is only about $20 trillion, and when legally enforceable bilateral netting agreements is taken into account, the gross derivatives exposure falls to $3.7 trillion.

What happens if the commercial bank becomes bankrupt? All the four outstanding derivative trades with the commercial bank will cease to exist. If there are other OTC derivative trades the corporate has with the commercial bank that are not hedged, it must seek another bank to enter into a similar trade to hedge its exposures. The same thing would also apply to the universal bank or foreign bank. Of concern to the corporate will be any cash or securities collateral it has provided to the commercial bank to meet initial and variation margin payments. This will have to be recovered through general bankruptcy proceedings if the collateral assets were not segregated from other assets of the commercial bank. Mitigating such counterparty risk in OTC derivative markets is engineered in the reform agenda by mandating central clearing of these trades. The entity that performs the central clearing of derivatives trades is called central counterparty (CCP). Examples of CCPs include LCH.Clearnet Ltd, Eurex Clearing and CME Clearing.

Let us revisit the interest rate swap trade of the corporate with the commercial bank. In the original trade the commercial bank was the counterparty to the corporate. Such a transaction would fall under the category of non-centrally cleared trade. In a centrally cleared derivatives trade, the commercial bank will simply act as an agent to facilitate this trade to be done with a CCP to which it has direct access. The terminology used is that the commercial bank is acting as a clearing member of the CCP. By shifting this trade to a CCP, the commercial bank and the corporate have no credit risk exposure with each other. For this to happen, the commercial bank will identify the universal bank as a willing counterparty to the trade without revealing the identity of its client.

Once the counterparty to the derivatives trade has been identified, the CCP becomes the only counterparty to which both the corporate and the universal bank have credit exposure to. This can be done through an open offer system where the CCP is automatically and immediately interposed in a transaction at the moment the buyer and seller agree on the terms. There will be no contractual relationship between the original counterparties to the trade in an open offer system. An alternative legal concept that allows the CCP to become counterparty to the trade is through novation. Under novation, the original contract between the buyer and seller is cancelled and replaced by two new contracts with the CCP so that the credit risk between the original counterparties to the trade ceases to exist.

An important benefit of CCP-cleared derivative trades is that it eliminates the multiple links among the market participants. Risks, however, become more concentrated with the CCP, but oversight arrangements, risk management principles, and capital requirements have all been strengthened to make CCPs safer. Let me now briefly discuss the types of OTC derivative transactions that require mandatory central clearing. That is, those for which the counterparty to the trade should be a CCP.

The language used by regulators is that standardised OTC derivatives should be centrally cleared. What are standardised derivatives? The interest rate swap transactions I mentioned above would, for example, fall under standardised derivatives. If the corporate had entered into a different trade where the contract would only commence in two months' time and the term of the interest rate swap is 3 years and 8 months, then this trade would be classified as non-standard OTC derivatives trade. This would have to be negotiated bilaterally, and regulators refer to this as a non-centrally cleared trade.

A credit default swap (CDS) contract referencing a traded bond index would be classified as a standardised product. On the other hand, if a client wants the bank to offer a CDS on a small customised portfolio of corporate bonds, this would fall under non-standardised derivatives trade. Many options traded on government bonds, such as those with 1 month or 3 month maturities, would also be seen as a standardised derivatives contract. But such contracts are usually traded on exchanges so that they are not targeted for central clearing. Most FX derivatives contracts would also fall under standardised derivatives, but they have been currently excluded from mandatory central clearing requirements. For this reason, only about 2 percent of FX derivatives are centrally cleared whereas about 75 percent of interest rate derivatives are centrally cleared as of mid-2016.

Beyond reducing the interconnections among market participants, central clearing of derivative trades helps a CCP to bring down the net exposure amounts considerably through multilateral netting across a broader pool of clearing members that trade with the CCP. Yet, to achieve this higher netting efficiency, CCPs will have to clear a wider range of OTC derivatives contracts rather than specialising in one product. Market forces are leading to this through horizontal integration of CCPs clearing different products. Horizontal integration refers to the formation of an integrated group that brings a number of clearing providers specialising in different derivative products under a common ownership structure. The reform agenda also requires OTC derivative trades to be reported to a trade repository so that regulators can have access to outstanding contracts to assess risk build up in this market segment. In the pre-crisis period, the lack of this information made risk assessment very difficult, and it complicated central bank decision-making when Lehman Brothers failed.

But how does central clearing of OTC derivatives reduce systemic risk in financial markets? There are multiple reasons how shifting OTC derivative trades to a CCP reduces system wide risks. They include: stricter rules on eligible collateral and margin requirements; identical rules for all market participants; safety of the posted initial and variation margins; and design features that allow outstanding trades of a defaulting clearing member to be shifted to other members. Let me provide a brief explanation of how these practices improve overall financial stability conditions.

In complying with the principles for financial market infrastructures, CCPs have to accept collateral with low credit, liquidity and market risks to manage credit exposure to its clearing members. Further, the applicable haircuts on collateral assets have to be conservative and calibrated to periods of stressed market conditions. The same applies to rules for determining initial margin requirements. CCPs are also required to carry out daily valuation of all outstanding derivative positions and collect variation margins at the same frequency to limit the build-up of exposures. Many of this may sound as common sense logic, but that logic failed in the run-up to the crisis for non-centrally cleared derivatives. By mandating central clearing of standardised derivatives and strengthening risk management rules at CCPs, the regulatory reforms are addressing important weaknesses uncovered in OTC derivatives markets.

The CCPs are also obliged to impose the same rules for every market participant irrespective of whether they have a triple-A rating or no rating. By contrast, banks that entered into bilateral derivatives trades with each other did not post initial margins. In some cases they had triggers to call for initial margins when the counterparty to the derivatives trade fell below a certain credit rating. The shift to central clearing of OTC derivatives trades reduces the burden on banks to monitor and manage the credit risks of these trades against many counterparties.

Another potential source for amplification of system wide risks is when market participants worry about their derivatives positions and posted collateral when their CCP clearing member is perceived to have solvency problems. To address this risk, CCPs are required to have segregation and portability arrangements for the trades and collateral of a clearing member's customers. Further, the CCP is also required to maintain customer positions and collateral in individual customer accounts or in omnibus customer accounts. An omnibus account holds collateral belonging to all customers of a particular clearing member in commingled single account segregated from that of the clearing member. The objective is that the trades of a defaulting clearing member's customers can be immediately transferred to other members.

These reform initiatives in turn raise the question as to how safe CCPs themselves are. Indeed, some observers are questioning whether CCPs are now the too-big-to-fail institutions. Regulators take this criticism seriously and are trying to address this through enhanced supervisory oversight arrangements and by developing principles for financial market infrastructures that provide guidance on how to deal with a clearing member default. The various sources of funds that a CCP has to protect against a clearing members' default are the following: the collateral posted by the member as first line of defence; if this is inadequate, the contribution to the default fund made by the member is used; the next in line are the contributions to the default fund made by other clearing members; and finally the own capital of the CCP. Beyond this, recovery and resolution techniques are also being developed to support orderly wind down of failing CCPs.

A number of policy challenges, however, still remain. An important one is about liquidity provision to critical financial market infrastructures such as a CCP. Many CCPs around the world operate under a commercial license as opposed to a banking license. In the absence of a banking license, a CCP does not have access to central bank deposit facilities and liquidity in times of stress. In this case, liquidity support can only be provided indirectly through a major bank, which in a systemic crisis can create some challenges. A more pressing question is how a CCP that clears OTC derivative trades denominated in multiple currencies may have adequate liquidity backstop arrangements in all those currencies. For example, a CCP located in a financial centre like London would offer central clearing of OTC derivatives in multiple currencies. If a clearing member default causes a large liquidity demand for euro or US dollars, the Bank of England would have to source it from the ECB or the Federal Reserve. Much progress has been made in this area under central bank cooperation.

Discussions among central banks generally lead to the conclusion that CCPs are a provider of public good, and consistent with this role, their governance arrangements and operational frameworks should be like those of a utility. That is, promoting safety and ensuring uninterrupted services should be their primary goals rather than generating profits for shareholders that might compromise these goals. Achieving them will very much depend on the ownership structure of CCPs. When a majority of clearing members themselves become shareholders, they often tend to have greater incentives to steer the governance arrangements and risk management frameworks towards safety of the CCP. But there are several CCPs with independent ownership structure that may have a bias towards profit motive. Yet another variant is the CCP being owned by the government or the central bank (as in Russia) signalling that it is a critical market infrastructure.

Let me now revisit the point I made earlier on netting efficiency where I mentioned that when a CCP clears a single product, the netting efficiency may be lower than what is achievable under bilateral netting agreements between market participants and banks or prime brokers on non-centrally cleared OTC derivatives trades. This is likely to be the case for hedge funds that tend to deal in multiple products. But there are a number of institutional investors who are more likely to trade only one type of product. For example, pension funds may wish to increase the maturity of their bond holdings to better match the long maturities of their pension liabilities. The standard strategy pension funds would employ is to enter into a long-maturity interest rate swap transaction to receive fixed rate and pay floating rate. In this case the netting efficiency does not change whether it is centrally cleared or non-centrally cleared from the perspective of the pension fund. Any hedging transactions they implement in the equity markets are usually done through equity index futures that are exchange traded and will not be cleared through CCPs.

The main bottleneck to achieving higher netting efficiency of trades done through CCPs is by not mandating central clearing of FX derivatives. Around 75 percent of all OTC derivatives trading comprise interest rate swaps and FX derivatives. If FX derivatives were to be also centrally cleared, and CCPs offer interest rates and FX products for clearing, similar netting efficiency levels are likely to be achieved as with bilateral clearing arrangements. Difficulty in reaching international consensus on dealing with cross-border collateral backing FX swaps has been one factor that has so far kept FX derivatives out of central clearing requirements. However, changes in capital requirements for OTC derivatives transactions under Basel III, which I will discuss, are altering incentives for market participants to centrally clear some types of FX derivatives.

But before I discuss this, let us ask the following question: why is netting efficiency so important? That is because margin requirements for a broker-dealer or its client depend on the outstanding portfolio of trades with a CCP. The more diversification there is in the derivatives portfolio – which would be the case when more types of OTC instruments are traded – the less the initial margins to be posted as the net exposure is reduced. Diversification benefits in the netting set also reduces the variation margins to be exchanged. Higher netting efficiency therefore lowers the amount of collateral needed to back the OTC derivatives trades that are centrally cleared.

The importance of achieving higher netting efficiency differs between the buy-side firms and sell-side firms. For buy-side firms, such as asset managers and pension funds, meeting requirements on initial margins through their holdings of bonds or other assets is not a problem. They have to do this anyway even if the derivative trades are non-centrally cleared. But a CCP may demand variation margin payments in cash, and managing these cash calls may require services of a custodian. Again, many asset managers already have such arrangements in place. Achieving a higher netting efficiency is not important for the business model of buy-side firms.

Much of the lobby against central clearing requirements and claims that it will create collateral shortages in financial markets comes from investment banks and broker-dealers who fall under the category of sell-side firms. They take as a reference the collateral needs they faced in the pre-crisis period when posting of initial margins were not expected from them. But that is no benchmark to measure against as the hidden cost of that practice to taxpayers has been enormous. Moreover, the posted collateral of market participants was often reused through securities financing transactions to fund bank assets or to take additional leverage. Central clearing requirements shifts the OTC derivative trades and posted collateral to a CCP resulting in loss of revenue to banks from the pre-crisis market practices. This is the main reason for discontentment which the dealer community presents as a threat of collateral shortage.

Estimates of additional collateral needs following changes in regulation that require both parties to an OTC derivatives trade to post initial margins vary widely. Many of these studies date back to 2012, and estimates vary from as low as $0.1 to as high as $3 trillion. There have been claims that there will be a huge shortage of high quality collateral assets when central clearing rules become binding.

Nothing of that sort has happened and liquidity in markets remains abundant so far going by the excess reserves held at central banks. Excess reserves held by US depository institutions at the Federal Reserve alone as of January 2017 has been close to $2 trillion. These excess reserves can be used to make initial and variation margin payments.

Yet, reducing collateral demand for OTC derivatives transactions under the new regulation are being explored by market participants. Towards this goal, various forms of CCP configurations are being contemplated to enhance multilateral netting efficiency. These include scope for establishing links or entering into cross-margining agreements between CCPs. For example, establishing a participant link will allow a CCP to operate in a manner similar to that of a clearing member with another CCP. Alternatively, two CCPs may establish a peer-to-peer link to broaden both the range of instruments cleared and the pool of participants using the clearing services.

The advantage of such links is that it allows clearing members to join only one CCP rather than multiple CCPs to clear similar products. By reducing collateral fragmentation and broadening the participant base utilising the clearing services, improved multilateral netting benefits can be achieved leading to reduced aggregate collateral demand to meet margin requirements. But the safety of such linked CCPs clearing OTC derivative trades is still untested, and at this time there is no broad regulatory support for establishing these links particularly when they involve cross-border CCPs.

Given the reluctance of broker-dealers and investment banks to lose an important revenue source as a result of central clearing of OTC derivatives, one may wonder if this will lead to a rise in non-standardised products that will not be subject to mandatory central clearing requirements. After all, regulators and bankers are constantly involved in a cat-and-mouse game. This time, however, the regulatory net has been cast wider and tighter. The Basel III rules on capital regulation for OTC derivatives exposures have been strengthened significantly, and at the same time, it incentivises banks to offer standardised OTC derivatives products to clients that will be subject to central clearing. Let me now discuss the main reforms in this market segment.

Underestimation of the potential losses from exposures to credit and market risks in the pre-crisis period was a general phenomenon. Post mortem of the sources of such risk underestimation in the OTC derivatives market have revealed that the method of calculation of the exposure at default (EAD) on outstanding derivative trades with a counterparty was flawed. This exposure amount, which used in the formula for computing capital charges, was calculated under Basel II based on either a current exposure method or standardised method, both of which have come under criticism. To provide some insights on the weakness of the approach under Basel II, let me introduce the equation that was used to determine the EAD for OTC derivative trades with a counterparty.

EAD = (MV – CA + Add-on)

Here, MV is the net market value of outstanding derivative trades with a counterparty, CA is the collateral amount after taking into account bank-determined haircuts on posted collateral assets, and Add-on is the add-on for the potential future exposure of the outstanding OTC derivatives. That is, the add-on represents the potential change in value of the derivative trades during the period between the last exchange of collateral before default of the counterparty and replacement of these trades in the market. When effective bilateral netting arrangements are in place, all outstanding OTC derivatives contracts are valued at current market prices and a net replacement cost or net MV of all contracts is computed. The add-on is determined by multiplying the notional amount of the contracts with a supervisory factor for the derivatives instruments from a look-up table. For contracts maturing in less than 5 years, these supervisory factors were 0.5 percent for interest rate swaps, 5 percent for FX derivatives, and 8 percent for equity derivatives.

Let me take a simple example to illustrate the computation of the capital charge on an OTC derivatives contract under Basel II. Consider an interest rate swap contract maturing in 4 years where the bank will receive a fixed interest rate from a corporate and pay a floating interest rate to the corporate. Let the notional amount of the contract be $100 million and the current market value of the swap be $1 million. The add-on for this trade will be the notional amount ($100 million) multiplied by the supervisory factor for this trade, which is 0.5 percent. This gives the value of the add-on to be $0.5 million. Suppose the corporate had posted a collateral asset that is worth $1.6 million today and the applicable haircut is 5 percent. The value of the collateral amount after the haircut is $1.52 million. The market value of the swap minus the CA would be the net replacement cost for the bank if the corporate were to default, which is negative $0.52 million. When this figure is summed with the add-on, it will result in EAD in the above equation to be negative $0.02 million. In this case, the EAD will be set to zero and no capital charges for the OTC derivative exposure will arise under Basel II rules.

Under the revised Basel III regulation, the replacement cost (RC) for the trade is computed as the market value of the OTC contract minus the collateral assets posted to mitigate the risk exposure, which is not allowed to go below zero. That is, the RC will now be equal to MV of $1 million minus the CA of $1.52 million, and as this value is negative, RC will be set to zero. The EAD calculation under Basel III is given below.

$$EAD = 1.4 \times [RC = \max(MV - CA; 0) + \text{multiplier} \times \text{Add-on}]$$

The equation shows that the potential future exposure from the derivatives trade is now calculated separately as a multiplier times the add-on. The multiplier can go in extreme cases as low as 0.05 when the bank holds significant excess collateral amount that is not returned to the counterparty. In normal cases the multiplier is close to one. The game changer is that the replacement cost cannot go below zero and reduce the EAD value as it was possible under Basel II. This is a key piece of reform to create incentives for banks to clear centrally, which is further supported by assigning lower risk weights for exposures to a CCP.

The actual formula for EAD under Basel III separates the collateral assets into those that have been exchanged under variation margin payments and those that fall under net initial margins held. The CA in the above equation will correspond to the cumulative variation margin payments received over the life of the contract. But this is a detail that I will skip. Also, the complete formula for computing the add-on varies by the asset type of the OTC derivatives contract making it complex for a simple exposition, so I will not discuss this either. What is useful to mention here is that the supervisory scaling factors used to compute the add-on have been increased for equity and commodity derivatives. Specifically, for equity derivatives on indices like S&P 500 the factor is 20 percent, and for commodities the factor is 18 percent. For FX derivatives the supervisory factor is 4 percent whereas for interest rate derivatives it is 0.5 percent.

The question of interest to us here is how the regulatory reforms in Basel III will affect the capital charges for the interest rate swap contract I discussed earlier. For this example, calculations will show that the add-on is $1.81 million and the multiplier is one so that EAD is equal to $2.53 million using the above equation. The important point to note here is that the new formula makes under- and over-estimation of prices of derivatives contracts unimportant in determining capital charges. What matters is the notional amount of OTC derivatives contracts that are outstanding with a particular counterparty. This influences the amount of add-on and through this the EAD value. Room for manipulation to lower capital charges is simply not there.

Let us take the risk weight to be 50 percent representative of a typical counterparty to the swap trade. For such a counterparty, the risk-weighted asset for this exposure turns out to be $1.26 million (EAD times the risk weight). For an 8 percent minimum capital ratio requirement, the capital charge for this OTC derivative exposure would be $101,000. The bank would have to set aside at least this amount of capital to offer a non-centrally cleared OTC derivatives trade of $100 million notional amount comprising an interest rate swap to the counterparty. This capital requirement is roughly about 0.1 percent of the notional amount of the derivatives contract. Under Basel II, the bank would not be setting aside any capital to enter into this derivatives trade.

Following this simple example, many might be wondering what the amount of undercapitalisation of banks and broker-dealers would have been prior to the crisis that was linked to their OTC derivatives trading activities. One could also rephrase this question as follows. If Basel III standards for OTC derivatives capital charges were in place in 2007, how much additional capital banks and broker-dealers in aggregate would have had to hold for their derivatives exposures? It is possible to provide some estimates based on the example I presented.

A first insight we get from the example swap trade is that the notional amount of derivatives is an important determinant of capital charges for OTC derivatives under Basel III. As of December 2007 the notional amount of outstanding OTC derivatives was close to $600 trillion. Let us assume that of this amount, $500 trillion was non-centrally cleared. The risk weight for this aggregate derivatives exposure is likely to be lower than 50 percent assumed in the above example due to the large amount of interbank derivatives trading positions. To take this into account, let us reduce the notional amount to $300 trillion, which is to say that the average counterparty risk weight is 30 percent rather than 50 percent since risk weights for banks are lower. While no diversification benefits are allowed across asset classes when computing the aggregate add-on, there are some diversification benefits within asset classes in the Basel formula leading to a reduction in the effective notional amount by 20 to 25 percent. This reduces the effective notional amount outstanding of non-cleared derivatives transactions to between $225 and $240 trillion. Following the example calculation above, applying a 0.1 percent capital requirement on the effective notional amount outstanding translates to additional capital needs of $225 to $240 billion. If banks had been complying with Basel III standards for capital requirements on their OTC derivatives transactions in 2007, then the global banking system would have needed additional capital to the tune of $250 billion for supporting their derivatives trading activities.

The incentives to centrally clear OTC derivative trades is being created by offering banks a significant reduction in applicable risk weights for exposures to CCPs. Specifically, when a bank is clearing a derivatives trade through a qualifying CCP – meaning, the CCP has been approved by regulators as meeting the principles for financial market infrastructures – the risk weight for the CCP is 2 percent. This value is 15 times lower than the 30 percent average risk weight that I used to compute the capital requirements in the previous example using Basel III rules. The formula for computing the EAD value remains the same as for non-centrally cleared trades. If all the OTC derivative trades are assumed to be cleared through CCPs, the capital requirements on these trades for the global banking system will be only about $20 billion. The netting efficiency level does not matter for capital charges, and as diversification benefits to reduce effective notional amounts can be reaped only within an asset class, CCPs do not have to clear multiple products to lower total capital charges on centrally cleared trades. This is the incentive structure being created under Basel III to shift OTC derivative trades towards CCPs.

So why are banks complaining about mandatory central clearing requirements on standardised OTC derivatives? The real reason, as I mentioned earlier, is the loss of revenue to banks from the shifting of posted collateral on these trades to CCPs or custodians. These collateral assets are not any more available to banks to reuse in securities financing transactions to raise cheap funding. But from a policy perspective, this is needed to reduce leverage in the financial system and to force banks to seek more resilient sources of funding which is monitored under the liquidity regulation standards.

Recovering collateral assets posted with Lehman Brothers that were backing securities financing and OTC derivatives transaction after bankruptcy was a major challenge that contributed to and amplified system-wide risks. Basel III standards are now designed to promote practices that support unhindered access to posted collateral when a counterparty defaults. This is done by enforcing additional capital requirements on banks when the collateral assets they post to CCPs or a custodian are not held in a bankruptcy remote manner.

If the bankruptcy remote condition is not met, collateral assets posted by the bank to the CCP on its own behalf and on its client behalf as a clearing member will face a capital charge estimated at 2 percent risk weight. For example, if $100 million of collateral assets (backing the bank's own derivatives trades and its client trades) are held without meeting the bankruptcy remote criterion at the CCP, the bank will have to set aside $0.16 million in capital ($0.16 = 100×2%×8%). This creates incentives for banks to play the role of policemen in ensuring that CCPs hold the collateral assets in ways that would ensure segregation and portability to another market provider if the CCP were to default.

For completeness, let me also mention here that banks will face some capital charges on the default fund that they hold with CCPs. In the extreme case when the bank is the only clearing member of the CCP, the default fund exposure will face 20 percent risk weight. If the volume of clearing the bank does with the CCP is insignificant compared to other members, the risk weight for the default fund exposure will be close to 2 percent.

There are also other sweeteners to encourage banks to clear derivative trades through a CCP. This is the time period applicable for determining haircuts on collateral assets. When the number of trades with a counterparty exceeds 5000, the haircuts on the collateral assets have to be determined assuming a 20-day holding period. This rule does not apply to CCP trades, and the holding period to be used for trades with CCPs is only 10-days. In practical terms this means that a 1 percent haircut on a collateral asset posted to a CCP will increase to 1.4 percent when it is posted with another counterparty with which the bank has lots of outstanding derivative trades.

Let me sum up by saying that Basel III standards use many levers to nudge banks to centrally clear OTC derivatives. As CCPs tend to clear only standardised derivative products, meaning plain vanilla products in trader jargon, one can say that regulatory reforms in the OTC derivatives market have been designed to discourage banks from trading and offering complex products to their clients. This is a big reform that directly affects investment banking revenues because the more complex the derivatives product, the more premium banks can charge their clients.

CHAPTER ELEVEN

BANK RESOLUTION

The importance of banks in payments and settlements of transactions, in financing of the economy, and in offering redeemable deposits to retail and corporate clients means that their continued operation is vital to authorities and the government. For this reason, governments have been forced to rescue banks using taxpayer funds when their solvency has come under threat. Such taxpayer-funded rescues are referred to as government bailout of banks. The bailout costs for UK taxpayers during the period 2008–13 have been about 6.3 percent of GDP. For taxpayers in the euro area, the bailout costs in the same period were 5.1 percent of GDP.

The public anger at the recklessness of bank's risk management practices leading to large losses that fell on taxpayers' shoulders forced G20 Leaders during their September 2009 Summit to commit to reforming the financial architecture and to ensure that under the redesigned rules taxpayers do not have to pay for the misadventures of banks. Towards this goal they agreed that regulatory authorities coordinated by the Financial Stability Board (FSB) will develop tools and frameworks for the effective resolution of financial groups to help mitigate the disruption of financial institution failures and reduce moral hazard in the future.

The reforms I presented so far under micro- and macroprudential regulation are intended to reduce the probability of failure of banks by mandating them to hold both higher levels of capital as well as better quality capital that is loss-absorbing when adverse scenarios materialise. Capital surcharges for systemically important financial institutions (SIFIs) are intended to provide additional safety margins. The reforms in OTC derivatives markets attempt to reduce panic and contagion in financial markets when a major derivatives trading firm comes under stress.

Yet in a market economy, the failure of a large bank – however low the probability of that event might be – cannot be ruled out. Moreover, when a large shock – be it economic, political, risk management failure or natural catastrophe – wipes out a significant amount of bank capital, the banking operations will have to be reorganised by letting some critical operations to continue while others are being dismantled. Coping with the failure of SIFIs without taxpayer solvency support is another major regulatory reform delivered as part of the overhaul of the financial architecture. Many in the central banking community consider the bank resolution regime to be the big structural reform in the financial sector after the Glass-Steagall Act that was introduced in 1933 to separate investment banking and commercial banking activities.

Before I discuss the efforts being taken to make non-viable banks resolvable, let me begin with an example to provide context to where bank resolution fits within the bigger scheme of post-crisis financial reforms. We are all aware of speed cameras installed in many locations on the highway as a means to reduce accidents by monitoring and punishing over-speeding drivers. The increase in the capital requirements for banks can be regarded as installing more of these speed cameras. Introducing mobile police patrols correspond to additional measures that include liquidity regulation and leverage ratio constraints.

But the law enforcement authorities can go a step further and require occupants in a car to wear their seat belts. And they can also require every car to be equipped with airbags to reduce serious injuries if accidents were still to occur. At the same time, modern cars protect drivers and passengers from the impact of an accident by using crumple zones to absorb crash energy. The bank resolution regime can be seen as the regulatory safety features for a bank that crashes to ensure that its important passengers – deposit holders, small and medium-sized enterprises dependent on bank financing, counterparties to derivative trades, and other critical payment system functions – can walk out and board another vehicle without major disruption to the traffic in the financial highways.

In a nutshell, the bank resolution regime instructs banks how they should be structured and operated so that the societal role of banks as a source of strength for financing real economic activities dominates shareholder interests. But it goes a step further in some adverse states of the world by subordinating the interests of certain bank creditors to the goal of safeguarding financial stability when it is being threatened. This raises the question as to whether an agency appointed by the state or the judiciary should be responsible for the orderly resolution of systemically important banks that meet these broader goals.

In normal circumstances, the interests of liability holders in a failing corporation are settled in bankruptcy courts. Unfortunately, bankruptcy proceedings in a court are more narrowly focused on interests of private creditors with complete disregard for the negative spillovers these court rulings may have for the broader economy and ultimately the taxpayers. The US court ruling in favour of holdout investors in Argentinian debt is a case in point. Seen from a financial stability perspective, it was a bad decision. But in defence of the judgment, the court has no obligation to weigh in adverse spillovers to the economy and is also not the competent authority to make this assessment.

Court-driven bankruptcy proceedings also tend to rely on imposing temporary stays on financial contracts so that creditors can negotiate a viable recovery plan for the firm. This would be the case in the US when invoking the Chapter 11 bankruptcy proceedings. But it is hard to imagine how imposing stays on outstanding repo trades and OTC derivatives contracts of a large bank holding company will foster financial stability. If anything, they will amplify financial instability by bringing trading in these markets to a halt.

There are further complications when a SIFI with large cross-border operations has to be resolved through bankruptcy as the Lehman Brothers case demonstrated. Specifically, a court ruling in one jurisdiction may force courts in other jurisdictions to ring fence assets of the subsidiaries of the bank and close down their operations. Because judges cannot enter into ex ante agreements with their counterparts in other countries, a court-driven bankruptcy process for large bank holding companies can be lengthy, complicated and impose significant economic costs when they are narrowly focused on the interests of a few creditors.

These considerations led authorities working under the FSB charter to recommend to governments to setup a resolution authority to be responsible for bank resolution. Under this plan, the resolution authority does not have direct responsibility for banking supervision. Many central banks have assumed the role of resolution authority and have established an independent division to be responsible for bank resolution. Through existing frameworks for central bank cooperation, resolution authorities can enter into ex ante commitments with their cross-border counterparts to share information on banks having a global footprint so that when their solvency comes under threat, authorities have a plan and a communication channel to deal with it. The key attributes for effective resolution regimes presented by the FSB recommends such cross-border cooperation agreements between resolution authorities to be established.

Many might wonder what this new bank resolution regime offers given that failing banks have been successfully dealt with in the past. For example, the Federal Deposit Insurance Corporation (FDIC) in the United States has been handling the resolution of failed depository institutions with domestic operations. The simple answer to the question why we need this new regime is that it is designed to facilitate resolution of even large banks with cross-border operations to take place without recourse to taxpayer money. But there is much more detail as to why the existing framework is insufficient or incapable of resolving large banks in an ever more interconnected global financial market place. I will take this question first and subsequently discuss what the new regime offers as practical solutions to bank resolution drawing on many of the lessons learned during the crisis.

For convenience, I will focus on the pre-crisis FDIC model for resolving problem banks. The resolution method most commonly used is called the Purchase and Assumption (P&A). This involves identifying a healthy bank willing to purchase the good assets of the failed bank and to take over the deposit and senior bond liabilities. Because taking over the new depositors by the bank has a franchise value, the FDIC charges a premium when transferring them to the acquiring bank. This partly pays for the resolution costs, and if the value of assets fall short of insured deposits transferred, the deposit insurance fund makes a compensating payment. The poor quality and non-performing assets are taken over by the FDIC – called receivership – and are progressively liquidated. Any residual values on these assets after deducting expenses incurred are distributed to remaining creditors and shareholders according to their claims hierarchy. This requires a court-driven bankruptcy proceeding to impose losses on creditors and shareholders.

What happens if a bank willing to acquire the assets cannot be found? In this case the FDIC takes over temporarily the operations of the bank. This will allow the bank to continue its operations even if it is in negative equity. As vital banking operations continue, the FDIC does a proper valuation of the assets, and determines which assets and liabilities will be taken into receivership and residual claims on the liabilities settled through bankruptcy proceedings. The remaining parts of the bank, which is operated as a temporary bridge bank, will have to be subsequently sold to another bank.

It does not require much imagination to conclude that this resolution approach will not work for resolving large bank holding companies like Bank of America or Citibank. This is not a theoretical question but a practical one that authorities were confronted with in the case of Citibank after the Lehman Brothers bankruptcy. Prior to the crisis, the FDIC's receivership authorities were limited to federally insured banks and thrift institutions. There was no authority to place a holding company or affiliates of an insured institution into FDIC receivership.

Even if the authorisation had existed, no bank can take on the task of valuing the huge balance sheet and complex securities and derivatives holdings of a large bank holding company in a short time. That is, it is not feasible to split the Citibank assets into good and bad assets or critical and non-critical parts and also assign appropriate values for them before transferring an equivalent amount of deposit liabilities. Further complications will arise as to whether FDIC will compensate depositors in foreign branches or subsidiaries of Citibank as per the US deposit insurance legislation.

This will create a bank depositor run in foreign branches and subsidiaries of the bank. Alternatively, putting a moratorium on payments on its outstanding liabilities would imply a Chapter 11 type bankruptcy filing. That decision would trigger a complete freeze of bank funding markets. To put it bluntly, the Federal Reserve and the US Treasury would not have an alternative option to bailing out Citibank in the old resolution regime.

The major problem with the old regime was that there was no agreed framework for resolution of cross-border banks. At the same time, large systemically important domestic banks also posed great risks to taxpayers if they failed. Moreover, imposing losses on shareholders and bank creditors required going through a lengthy court-driven settlement process in the old regime. Avoiding this route and restoring critical banking operations usually meant taxpayer funded bailout was the only option. The new bank resolution regime cracks this hard nut through an internationally agreed framework to impose losses on shareholders and creditors without triggering a bankruptcy proceeding.

To reach an international agreement on bank resolution regimes, the FSB presents a set of key attributes that need to be met to make financial institutions with cross-border operations resolvable without disrupting the functioning of global financial markets. Each jurisdiction has transformed these key attributes into legislation that has already entered into force in major financial centres. I will briefly present the essential features of these attributes and then discuss how the resolution regime forces changes to bank business models as well as the composition and type of bank liabilities.

First and foremost, the key attributes require each jurisdiction to have a designated resolution authority for exercising the resolution powers over financial firms within the scope of the resolution regime. Those resolution powers include among others the following: remove and replace senior management of the firm; appoint an administrator to manage the firm; operate and resolve the firm, including powers to terminate contracts, purchase or sell assets and write down debt; override rights of shareholders of firm in resolution; to transfer selected assets and liabilities to a third party or to a newly established bridge institution without requiring consent of any interested party; and to put a stay on creditor actions to attach assets while protecting the enforcement of eligible netting and collateral agreements.

The key attributes gives creditors the right to seek compensation if they would have received more through liquidation of the firm under the applicable insolvency regime rather than using resolution tools. But the attributes disallow for judicial actions that could constrain the implementation of, or result in the reversal of, measures taken by resolution authorities in good faith. The resolution authority is also to be empowered with resolution powers over local branches of foreign firm and to support a resolution carried out by a foreign authority that may require transfer of property and assets located in its jurisdiction to a bridge institution. This is part of the cross-border cooperation arrangements foreseen in the key attributes.

Considering that funding of firms in resolution is an important prerequisite to operationalise the resolution regime, the key attributes requires privately financed deposit insurance or resolution funds to be in place. This is to ensure that authorities are not constrained to rely on public or bailout funds as a means to resolve failing institutions. Beyond this, there are many legal terminologies accompanying the key attributes given that in achieving the broader goals of safeguarding financial stability and mitigating adverse economic spillover, the rights of private creditors have to be temporarily suspended. But I will skip these details.

Among the powers given to the resolution authority, I mentioned the transfer of selected assets and liabilities to a third party or bridge bank. This is likely to bring up the following question: What crystal ball does the resolution authority possess to be able to separate the assets into good and bad ones? After all, this was one of the bottlenecks I pointed out why large banks cannot be resolved using the tools of the old regime. The FSB's key attributes delivers this crystal ball to resolution authorities by requiring an ongoing process for recovery and resolution planning of domestically as well as globally systemically important financial institutions to be put in place. This plan is to be drawn up by the financial institution itself taking into consideration its cross-border operations and intra-group financial support arrangements. The regulatory jargon for this recovery and resolution plan to be submitted is called "Living Will". The concept is similar to the "Last Will" written by someone as regards how his or her estate is to be broken up and shared among the dependents.

By requiring the senior management of the firm themselves to draw up the Living Will forces them to restructure business operations if they realise that their recovery and resolution plans may not be approved by supervisory and resolution authorities. Particularly when cross-border operations are involved, the form of parent-subsidiary support provided can affect how a foreign subsidiary would be resolved, and consequently, as to how implied liabilities of that support will be recognised ex ante. In the old regime, senior management had no incentive or obligation to worry about the firm if it becomes non-viable. This allowed often unsustainable business practices to be pursued during economic expansions for the sake of immediate management rewards.

Typical recovery plans for a bank would include measures to reduce the risk profile of the bank and conserving capital by suspending dividend payments, as well as options such as sale of business lines and restructuring of liabilities. Resolution plans, on the other hand, tend to be much more comprehensive. Its main aim is to make the resolution of the bank or financial firm feasible without serious disruption to critical services and without exposing taxpayers to loss. That requires the plan to identify the critical business functions along with suitable resolution options to preserve those functions or wind them down in an orderly fashion. In addition, the plans should provide for actions to protect insured depositors and ensure the quick return of segregated client assets held.

In circumstances where the supervisory or resolution authorities have serious concerns about the resolvability of the bank based on the plans submitted by the bank management, they are empowered to do the following. Authorities can instruct the senior management to adopt changes to the banks' business practices, structure or organisation in order to reduce the complexity and cost of resolution. To put it mildly, authorities can tell the senior management how they should be running their banking business in the broader interests of safeguarding financial stability and reducing economic costs associated with bank failures.

How do these key attributes facilitate effective resolution of financial firms in practice? This would be the question in the minds of non-experts as much of what I said sounds very theoretical. Making this theory work in practice requires firms to issue a certain amount of debt which is subject to statutory bail-in. This debt is called the gone-concern loss-absorbing capacity that comprises subordinated bonds or senior unsecured bonds. That is, if a bank has issued senior unsecured bonds that can be redeemed at $100 at maturity, a part or all of the value of the bonds can be converted into bank equity. If, for example, only $20 is converted into equity, the remaining $80 will be the new redeemable value of the bond at maturity. If the bond has a junior claim, the full value of the bond is usually converted into equity. Under resolution, the original bank equity holders are written off or will become residual claimants in the assets of the firm that are being liquidated. Going back to the car example I introduced, the bail-in debt is the crumple zone regulatory authorities have introduced to avoid injuries to the financial system if accidents were to occur.

An important legal pre-condition to be met in achieving the above goal is that the statutory bail-in of these bonds – a decision that is imposed by resolution authorities – should not trigger cross-default clauses in other bank liabilities. At the same time, banks are discouraged to hold debt issued by other banks to reduce financial interdependencies. Capital requirements under Pillar 2 can be used by supervisors as a deterrent. Beyond this, bonds that are issued in foreign jurisdictions will have to include legal clauses that allow resolution authorities to bail-in those bonds without the right being granted to holders of the bonds to contest these decisions in court. Where this debt with loss-absorbing capacity is to be held depends on the type of resolution strategy adopted by the bank or financial firm. The FSB proposal includes two resolution strategies – the single point of entry (SPE) and the multiple point of entry (MPE).

The SPE resolution strategy is structured such that the holding company is responsible for absorbing the losses of its subsidiaries and branches distributed globally. That means the consolidated balance sheet of the entire group will determine the amount of loss-absorbing capacity that is to be held at the holding company level. The MPE strategy, as the name suggests, is structured to allow regional subgroups or foreign country subsidiaries to be resolved in a decentralised manner. While the host authorities of banks that opt for a MPE resolution strategy will have responsibility for resolution, the home authority where the group holding company is located has a role in ensuring that the MPE strategy is well coordinated and does not create risks to the group as a whole. Firms that opt for MPE strategy will have to hold the appropriate loss-absorbing capacity at the respective sub-group or subsidiary level which will be subject to resolution.

Operational challenges to resolution under the MPE strategy can arise from intra-group dependencies that might exist. This is often the case in areas of IT services that could include reliance on group level risk management functions and software solutions. Proper resolution planning will be needed in these cases to ensure continuity of these services during the transition phase when resolution tools are applied. This may require entering into enforceable contracts ex ante to avoid disruption to these services. Ultimately, a group's choice of financial and operational structures for its subsidiaries and branches will influence the home and host authorities as to whether the group will require a SPE or a MPE resolution strategy so that resolution plans can be prepared accordingly. This brings me to the next topic of how the bank resolution regime is influencing or altering bank business models and legal structures.

A global bank operating in different jurisdictions might choose a legal structure that is either a branch or a subsidiary form. The branch form does not have a standalone legal personality and is reliant on the parent bank for capital, liquidity and other support functions. A subsidiary, on the other hand, is an independent legal entity backed by its own capital and liquidity facilities and tends to be funded locally. The business model pursued by the banking group may itself influence the legal form under which it operates in other jurisdictions.

For example, in large financial centres, the holding company may prefer to setup a branch to raise cheaper wholesale funding for the group as a whole. A number of other factors such as high tax regime in the host country, focus on investment banking rather than retail banking, and low country risk are also likely to favour operation through branches. In cases where the holding company focuses on retail banking activities and supports a more decentralised business model, subsidiaries are usually favoured. However, with the introduction of legislation on bank resolution in many countries now, the business model chosen influences the type of resolution strategy that is applicable. If, for instance, the holding company provides significant intragroup loans to its branches and subsidiaries, then the regulatory authorities will want a SPE resolution strategy. If the holding company would rather prefer to present a MPE resolution strategy, it would have to restructure its business operations so that the subsidiaries or subgroups become standalone entities that can be resolved independently.

Regulatory authorities may also express preference for a particular resolution strategy. The FDIC under Title II of the Dodd-Frank Act has chosen SPE as the preferred resolution strategy for US SIFIs. This allows the business model of the group to be more centralised and benefit from economy of scale on raising debt or provision of intragroup liquidity. The SPE strategy also reduces the incentives to ring-fence assets of branches and subsidiaries in foreign jurisdictions by the host authorities.

In the EU, the bank recovery and resolution directive (BRRD) does not express a preferred strategy. Still, resolution authorities can impose changes to the legal structure of banks. Many Spanish banks with cross-border operations in Latin America have structured their business model to be more compliant with MPE resolution plan. It is also the preferred strategy of Spanish regulatory authorities to mitigate contagion from its Latin American subsidiaries as well as those of the host authorities. Consequently, the cross-border banking operations of large Spanish banks in non-EU countries are organised as standalone subsidiaries. In Switzerland, the regulatory authorities have expressed a clear preference for SPE strategy for resolution of the two largest banks. This would dictate how the cross-border business lines are organised, funded and operated.

An important prerequisite for effective resolution is clarity on creditor hierarchy. This is also important from a creditor perspective to be able to price different types of bank debt depending on the level of losses from the subordination they embed. The standard form of subordination used in corporate finance is the contractual subordination. As the name indicates, the creditor and debtor agree contractually whether the debt claims on a particular instrument will rank higher or lower in terms of hierarchy during the claims process under insolvency of the firm. For example, claims on senior unsecured debt are paid in full before junior subordinated debt is repaid. A contingent convertible debt will convert to equity at the contractually set trigger level and is below subordinated debt in seniority.

The introduction of a bank resolution regime creates an additional layer of subordination called statutory subordination by requiring a certain amount of debt instruments to be available for bail-in. That is, they can be converted into equity without entering into bankruptcy proceedings. The statutory subordination, however, will have to respect the contractual subordination hierarchy of the various bank liabilities. In the old regime when non-viable banks were taken through bankruptcy proceedings, uninsured deposits were ranked at the same level of hierarchy as unsecured bank bonds. Clearly, this poses many challenges and concerns for retail as well as for small and medium-sized enterprises (SMEs) about the safety of their deposits. Even for large corporates it will be a major problem if their operational balances are ranked at the same level as unsecured bank bonds under statutory bail-in. Lack of clarity on the statutory subordination of uninsured deposits can therefore pose challenges to financial stability by triggering traditional depositor runs when a bank is being seen as a candidate for resolution.

To address this, regulatory authorities have provided more clarity on the hierarchy of bank liabilities under bail-in. In the EU, Member States are required to ensure that in their national law governing normal insolvency proceedings, eligible deposits from natural persons and SMEs which exceed the insured level are ranked more senior to claims of ordinary unsecured and non-preferred creditors. Germany has introduced an additional category of subordinated senior debt through statutory subordination to other operational bank liabilities. France has created a non-preferred senior debt category through contractual subordination, which banks will have to issue as bail-in debt. In the US, all deposit holders are treated as preferred creditors so that they rank more senior to claims on unsecured bank debt.

Another category of subordination can be introduced through structural subordination. This becomes important under the SPE resolution strategy where the shareholders and external creditors of the pure holding company will be the first to bear the losses. The creditors of the operating subsidiary will be protected if the holding company has sufficient loss-absorbing capacity. This brings up the question as to how much loss-absorbing capacity banks will have to hold.

To answer this, I will focus on the FSB standards that are set for global systemically important banks (GSIBs) on loss-absorbing and recapitalisation capacity in resolution. The standards are set in terms of the total loss-absorbing capacity (TLAC) GSIBs have to hold at the level of the resolution entity. The instruments that qualify towards TLAC are those that fall under the categories Tier 1 and Tier 2, and other debt securities. But these debt securities must be subordinated to any excluded liabilities. The excluded liabilities include among others insured deposits, deposits with original maturity of less than one year, and liabilities arising from derivatives contracts. Because TLAC standard is seen as a Pillar 1 requirement under Basel III rules, instruments that are intended to meet regulatory capital buffers, such as countercyclical and systemically important buffers, cannot be included in TLAC.

FSB standards set the minimum requirements for TLAC as 16 percent of risk-weighted assets of the bank, which become effective from January 2019. If we exclude the minimum capital ratio requirements of 8 percent under Pillar 1, TLAC sets the minimum bail-in instruments to be held at 8 percent of risk-weighted assets. Debt instruments that qualify towards TLAC should have a residual maturity of more than one year. If the instruments have a residual maturity of less than two years, then only 50 percent of the amount that is outstanding count towards TLAC. This encourages banks to issue long-term debt instruments that are contractually subordinated to ensure bail-in debt is available if the institution faces a solvency crisis.

To reduce interconnectedness among banks, holdings of capital instruments and bail-in debt of another bank are discouraged. Banks are allowed to hold amounts up to 10 percent of their own common equity in TLAC instruments issued by other banks. Amounts held that exceed this threshold have to be deducted directly from their Tier 1 or Tier 2 capital depending on what type of instrument is being held. Beyond this, GSIBs are allowed to hold in its trading book TLAC instruments issued by other banks up to 5 percent of its common equity to facilitate market making activities. Similar rules also apply to non-GSIBs when they hold eligible TLAC instruments issued by other banks. This serves as a strong deterrent and ensures that TLAC instruments cannot be a channel for contagion among large banking groups.

To provide practical insights into how the standards set by global regulatory bodies for bank resolution is transformed into enforceable national legislation, I will highlight key features of the EU and US implementations. In the EU, FSBs' key attributes are implemented through the BRRD. This directive has been transposed into national legislation in the EU Member States.

An important element of the BRRD is that the resolution tools are also meant to be applied to commercial banks which may not be categorised as GSIBs. To facilitate resolution of a more diverse group of banks, some departures from the key attributes relating to the requirement on loss-absorbing capacity and how it is to be quantified, as well as on resolution funding arrangements are made. Being broader in its remit so that a wider group of banks can be subject to resolution, the BRRD provides a useful piece of legislative blue print for many emerging market economies for drafting their national legislation on bank resolution.

The interesting and practical elements in BRRD are the resolution tools it provides and the resolution funding arrangements that are available to resolution authorities. I will therefore focus on these elements and also explain how the requirements on loss-absorbing capacity are set. The term used for loss-absorbing capacity in the EU directive is minimum requirements for own funds and eligible liabilities (MREL) which is the counterpart to TLAC.

In setting the loss-absorbing capacity, MREL is framed as a Pillar 2 requirement in contrast to Pillar 1 requirement under TLAC. This shift in focus provides authorities greater flexibility in dealing with banks with different business models and varying asset sizes so that MREL requirements can be allowed to differ across banks while better aligning it with the resolution planning process. Moreover, the amount of capital instruments and eligible liabilities for bail-in to be held are specified as a percent of total liabilities including own funds rather than risk-weighted assets in the current EU legislation. But there are now proposals from the European Banking Authority to set MREL requirements for banks as a share of risk-weighted assets to make it more comparable with the TLAC proposal.

Let me provide an example to illustrate how MREL requirements are set for banks. Consider bank A to be a medium-sized bank that has to meet 10.5 percent overall capital requirements as a share of risk-weighted assets (8 percent minimum capital requirements plus 2.5 percent capital buffer). If the risk-weighted assets amount to 40 percent of total liabilities including its common equity, the going-concern capital requirements amount to 4.2 percent of total liabilities. Assuming the bank carries out some critical functions that need to be preserved if the bank becomes non-viable, the resolution plan adopted might be to transfer these functions to a bridge bank and wind down the remaining assets and liabilities. Let us say that the critical functions to be transferred to the bridge bank constitute 50 percent of the risk-weighted assets. From the resolution authorities' point of view, bank A in its current form will have to maintain one-half of the 4.2 percent of total liabilities in recapitalisation instruments. This would result in MREL being set at 6.3 percent (4.2 percent plus 2.1 percent) of total liabilities including its capital instruments.

If MREL requirements were set as a share of risk-weighted assets to be held, then bank A will be required to maintain 15.7 percent of its risk-weighted assets towards MREL. What happens if risk-weighted assets of bank A are only 20 percent of total liabilities instead of 40 percent? In this case the MREL requirement for the bank is still 15.7 percent of risk-weighted assets, but as a share of total liabilities MREL will be only 3.1 percent. Although the amount 15.7 percent appears to be very similar to the 16 percent TLAC requirement, MREL includes in its calculation capital buffers that banks have to maintain. If we exclude these capital buffers, bank A will have to maintain 13.2 percent of risk-weighted assets as TLAC.

To resolve a non-viable bank, the BRRD provides resolution authorities with four tools. They include: the sale of business tool; the bridge institution tool; the asset separation tool; and the bail-in tool. The sale of business tool can be used for effecting the transfer of the whole or part of the banks' business to another institution. If there is no willing buyer, the resolution authorities can set up a bridge bank that is under public ownership until a willing buyer is found.

Under the bridge institution tool, non-performing assets and non-viable parts of the banks' business are separated and transferred together with liabilities that are eligible for bail-in to an asset management company which is also publicly owned. Following the proceeds of the asset sales, any residual value left after paying for the operating costs of the asset management company is distributed to shareholders and debt holders as per their creditor hierarchy. The bail-in resolution tool allows authorities to convert certain categories of debt into equity for recapitalising the bank if its continued operation is critical to safeguard financial stability. The BRRD allows the bail-in tool to be employed to resolve any bank, not just GSIBs, when the liquidation option for the bank is not seen as a viable strategy in the interests of financial stability.

The resolution tools mentioned above have to be applied before any external financial support is extended to an institution. Such external support can be provided through a resolution fund, which is complementary to the deposit guarantee fund that reimburses insured depositors. Like the deposit guarantee fund, the resolution fund is to be built up from contributions made by the banks themselves and is under control of public authorities. In circumstances where the application of the resolution tools cannot restore the capital requirements of a bank under resolution, the resources of the resolution fund can be used to meet the capital shortfall. Because the resolution fund is under a public authority, injection of capital to take an equity position in the bank under resolution will be treated as State aid in the EU framework. Preconditions for eligibility and limits to this State aid are therefore established. These include: writing down shareholder equity and converting to equity those liabilities that are eligible for bail-in so that collectively they comprise at least 8 percent of total liabilities and own funds of the bank; and restricting the contributions from the resolution fund to not exceed 5 percent of total liabilities of the bank under resolution.

To ensure the checks and balances are in place and oversight arrangements are appropriate and coordinated, the EU has established a Single Resolution Fund (SRF) to manage this process. The SRF is comprised of contributions from banks and some investment firms in 19 EU Member States. It is to be gradually built up to reach a target funding level of 1 percent of covered deposits of all banks in the participating Member States by end-2023. Under the current setup, contributions from banks in each Member State go into a separate and segregated resolution fund.

Going forward, the segregated resolution funds will be gradually merged into one fund by 2024 so that there is one fund – the SRF – that will provide resolution financing only to the extent necessary to ensure the effective application of the resolution tools. These financing arrangements include: to make loans to or purchase assets of the bank under resolution; to guarantee the assets or liabilities of the bank under resolution; to pay compensation to shareholders or creditors who incurred greater losses than under normal insolvency proceedings; and in exceptional circumstances make capital injections to the bank under resolution. Recognising that situations might arise where SRF resources are insufficient to support orderly resolution, a Loan Facility Agreement has been put in place to allow each Member State to provide a credit line to their national resolution fund compartment.

The effective resolution regime of the FSB is implemented in the US through Title II of Dodd-Frank Act. Under this Act, an Orderly Liquidation Authority (OLA) is established, which is effectively an agency-driven resolution process as an alternative to winding down a large failing financial institution through bankruptcy procedures. The OLA provides FDIC various powers that include establishing a bridge financial institution, to convert debt of the holding company eligible for bail-in to equity, and to provide temporary liquidity to the bridge institution when private sector options are unavailable.

In developing a resolution strategy, FDIC has favoured the SPE strategy. This would place the holding company of the bank into receivership while establishing a temporary bridge bank to hold and manage its critical operating subsidiaries for a limited period. The assets of the holding company would be transferred from the receivership to the bridge bank, whereas the liabilities of the holding company would be left in the receivership to cover the losses and expenses from the resolution process. Rule-making by the Federal Reserve will require US SIFIs to issue a minimum amount of long-term debt eligible for bail-in at the holding company level. The holding company's debt eligible for bail-in provides the means to capitalise the bridge bank and its subsidiaries. The resolution process ends when the bridge bank is wound down after the subsidiaries have been recapitalised or put to orderly liquidation.

The Dodd-Frank Act also provides for establishing an Orderly Liquidation Fund (OLF). The OLF is to provide a backup source of liquidity (and not capital) to the bridge bank if access to private funding markets for the bridge bank is disrupted. This provision is consistent with FSB's key attributes in contrast to the EU BRRD which creates scope for exceptional circumstances to arise to justify capital injections through the SRF to a bank under resolution. But there are other differences too. The SRF is pre-funded by collecting ex ante contributions from banks consistent with FSB key attributes, whereas the OLF provides for ex post levy on banks if there are losses to the OLF from liquidity support that cannot be recouped from the resolution process. Because there is no pre-funding, the OLF relies on a credit line from the US Treasury to provide the liquidity support.

CHAPTER TWELVE

CHALLENGES AHEAD

Financial markets are constantly evolving in response to various developments that impact it: shifts in investor preferences that influence demand for new products; improvements in information technology that bring new platforms for trade execution and order matching; and changes in regulation that may require fundamental overhaul of risk management practices. Notwithstanding the comprehensive regulatory reforms leading to a complete rewiring of the financial architecture, policy makers, politicians and public at large cannot claim it is mission accomplished in building a resilient financial system. Perhaps it will never be given the adaptations constantly taking place in the financial interlinkages even if the redesigned architecture has contributed significantly in moving towards this goal.

While implementation of the financial reforms is in an advanced stage of completion, regulators continue to explore new links through which risks can propagate in a highly interconnected global financial system. One of those areas of investigation is shadow banking that has been identified as an area of priority. But even in the regulated financial system, some have expressed concerns that changes in risk appetite and provision of liquidity to markets by the broker-dealer community resulting from of the regulatory reforms can be a channel for risk propagation. Many central banks are also still challenged to restore employment, growth and price stability targets to levels that their mandates require them to do. To reach these goals, central banks in advanced economies have been forced to resort to unconventional monetary policy measures that include purchasing assets and charging negative interest rates on excess reserves held by banks.

In this chapter I will review these developments and try to give my personal views on number of issues. One is on shadow banking where I will highlight why monitoring this sector will be a challenge for authorities given the diversity of entities that fall under this category. To keep the task manageable, one has to be very selective. The other is about banks' capacity and willingness to provide liquidity to markets in light of the reforms, and what risks if any this poses. I will then turn to two specific topics where I see material risks, one in the near term and another in the medium term. The near term risk I will focus on is the problems facing the banking sector in a number of euro area countries. Over the medium term, the risks to the financial system are likely to materialise from underfunded pension schemes as the risk of an extended period of low macroeconomic growth in advanced economies has not been fully factored into benefits design. I will provide some views on this even if pension reforms will be very difficult to implement.

One concern that has been raised in many forums is whether strengthened regulation and supervision of banks will lead to a shift in the credit intermediation activities to outside the regulated sector that have the potential to increase risks to financial stability. When these activities involve bank-like functions – maturity and liquidity transformation and leverage – the entities providing these services are called shadow banks. This is because non-bank entities pursuing these activities hold little or no capital in contrast to their regulated counterparts, which can be interpreted as a form of capital arbitrage.

Considerable efforts are now being taken to better understand the channels, instruments and business practices through which non-bank entities may pose risks or amplify risks to the financial system. The channels can be through interconnections between banks and non-banks; instruments can be those that result in imperfect credit risk transfer; and business practices can be those that allow liabilities to be subject to runs by offering demand deposit type features. The work on shadow banking is being coordinated by the FSB and it covers among others establishing criteria to identify shadow banks and determining their size. As of end-2014 the size of the global shadow banking sector is estimated to be around $36 trillion. This measure of size is based on identifying shadow banks using five economic functions or activities carried out them. These economic functions include: collective investment vehicles with features that make them susceptible to runs; loan provision that is dependent on short-term funding; intermediation in financial markets using client assets for secured funding or using short-term funding; facilitation of credit creation; and securitisation-based credit intermediation.

Typical entities that carry out these economic activities include the following: money market mutual funds; asset management firms offering bond funds to clients; credit and macro hedge funds; real estate funds; financing companies, leasing companies and consumer credit companies; broker-dealers; financial guarantors and credit insurance companies; and securitisation vehicles. This is a rather diverse group of entities with different business models making it a challenge to monitor their activities with the objective of identifying specific sources of risk that can amplify or contribute to financial instability. While monitoring and identifying economic activities that can contribute to financial instability from a policy angle is very important, flagging specific financial structures or types of trades that have the potential to amplify risks to the financial system is extremely difficult. These tasks require deep understanding of financial market practices including experience on the trading floor to be familiar with the financial market jargon, some knowledge of international accounting standards, deep understanding of risk management practices, the specific business model practices of very different entities, and the foresight to piece together how interactions across these areas can potentially contribute to financial instability.

Building capacity in central banks for carrying out these tasks is a daunting task. This requires very different skills compared to carrying out microprudential banking supervision which is largely rule based even if some discretionary decisions have to be taken by supervisors under Pillar 2 of Basel III. But my concern is that many normal business risks could be flagged as potential sources of financial stability risk depending on the level of understanding of those who monitor these activities. Let me provide some concrete examples for my source of concerns.

Let us assume that a client entrusts some funds to an asset manager offering an active management style to outperform an investment grade corporate bond benchmark. The asset manager performs the fiduciary duty of replicating the bond benchmark while seeking opportunities to outperform it. There is also a contractual agreement between the client and the asset manager regarding the fees that will be charged for managing the funds entrusted. If there are many corporate bond defaults and the prices of corporate bonds fall due to heightened macroeconomic risks, the net asset value of the clients' bond portfolio will fall in value. If many clients who have entrusted money with the asset manager to replicate the same benchmark in a comingled bond fund liquidate their funds due to rising risk, it can add to the price pressure on corporate bonds.

These price actions do not contribute to financial stability risk. Large and simultaneous withdrawals by retail and institutional clients from bond funds will exacerbate losses and amplify market volatility. The investors will have to bear those losses as they stem from their own decisions to invest in riskier and perhaps also less liquid assets. Mutual funds that offer these products are prohibited by regulation from taking on leverage to increase returns in normal times. Therefore, they cannot be borrowing from banks or raising short-term funds to invest in the corporate bond portfolio. One usually speaks of a run when the liability side of the balance sheet of a financial firm faces sudden and large redemptions. The assets under management are not consolidated in the balance sheet of financial firms offering third party asset management services and these assets are legally separated. The redemption claims are simply met through liquidation of assets with the gains or losses from the sales being passed to the investor.

What could be the channels for financial instability from actions of asset managers or mutual funds managing bond funds? One channel could be through a universal bank offering asset management services to its clients. When an adverse shock hits the corporate sector, the universal bank might use its trading book to buy the assets liquidated by its asset management clients to reduce sharp falls in the prices of those assets and forestall further client redemptions. The increased risk on the universal banks' balance sheet may turn out to be difficult to shed and lead to sharp fall in its share price. Regulators may be concerned about the risk such a scenario of events might subsequently pose to the financial system as a whole.

How realistic is this scenarios? In the pre-crisis period the demise of Bear Stearns was linked to such a scenario. The actions of BNP Paribas putting a moratorium on withdrawals from investment funds invested in subprime mortgages that the bank was managing led to broader risk spillovers into the financial system. But the post-crisis reforms have addressed this risk. Banks that do not consolidate off-balance sheet activities in its balance sheet will not be allowed to provide any form of support when the off-balance sheet vehicle, such as third-party asset management services, faces problems.

Another channel for risk contagion could be from large bilateral OTC derivatives trading positions held by asset management firms with an investment bank that faces a solvency crisis. This is the Lehman Brothers example that amplified risks through it prime brokerage and derivatives trading services provided to clients including asset managers. But the reforms in the derivatives market including the mandatory clearing of standardised derivative trades through a CCP have largely addressed this source of risk contagion.

A third source of risk can come from losses to client money due to either large operational errors or portfolio managers not respecting the risk guidelines in the asset management mandate. But this would fall under business risk and is also not a system-wide risk that will trigger contagion. Similarly, the inability of an asset manager to liquidate client portfolios in a short period of time due to poor market liquidity is a risk that the client has taken by deciding to invest in less liquid assets to increase long-term returns. Central banks may respond to market freezes to support market functioning, but this does not require close oversight of the activities of asset management firms. There is also a risk that such close oversight may create the wrong expectation that central banks will intervene to facilitate large redemption requests to safeguard financial stability as it was done to support US money market funds after the Lehman Brothers failure. What is needed is investor education and perhaps also explicit recognition by asset managers in their marketing material that large investor redemptions of particular portfolios can cause significant fall in the net asset value due to exposures to less liquid assets. Increasing redemption times on such portfolios would also help the liquidation process to be orderly.

A similar reasoning would apply to hedge fund activities even if some of their trading behaviour can amplify market volatility. Yet, increased market volatility forces investors and risk takers to be not complacent, and it also contributes to both reduced leverage and valuation of assets to be more conservative. To sum up, despite fixed income funds and credit hedge funds being categorised as shadow banks under FSBs' economic activities classification, I fail to see how their activities can pose bank-like systemic risks to the financial system.

Still, some nuances are needed as certain portfolio replication styles can be a cause for concern as new products are rolled out. One example is when an asset manager uses a synthetic portfolio to replicate the returns of a benchmark. That is, rather than buying the underlying assets to replicate the benchmark, the portfolio manager might enter into a non-centrally cleared total return swap with a broker-dealer or a universal bank to generate the returns of the benchmark. Such replication styles have been used in synthetic exchange traded funds (ETFs) to offer clients immediate liquidity for their portfolio holdings even when the underlying benchmarks were illiquid. These structures increase interconnectedness between asset managers and banks, and therefore can be a reason for greater scrutiny of such practices. Yet, this is a very narrow mandate for regulatory oversight within the asset management industry to look for structures that have potential to amplify financial risks. The same may be said of high frequency trading where scope for risk contagion to the financial markets may exist and warrant attention.

A question that often comes up is whether hedge funds' trading styles can compromise the resilience of the financial system. By trading more frequently in markets, hedge funds generally contribute to improved price discovery (that is, it helps establish the market price for financial assets) and market liquidity. Will not hedge funds amplify price falls and add to systemic risk as the LTCM episode demonstrated? The LTCM crisis was fuelled by excessive leverage being taken by the managers with funding provided by broker-dealers. Moreover, proprietary desks in many banks were replicating this trading strategy resulting in similar positions being built up across the industry, which in hindsight was a major contributing factor to increased systemic risk. Following post-crisis reforms, haircuts on assets for repo trades have been raised, variation margin payments have to be made daily, and banks themselves cannot engage in the proprietary trading activities under the US Volcker rule. If incoming governments do not rewind the regulatory reform tape, a repeat of events of similar depth and reach through a hedge fund trading strategy is unlikely.

This brings up the following question: What forms of shadow banks can potentially lead to regional or global financial system being less resilient and where are they located? In advanced economies, the classical shadow banks are money market mutual funds that offer constant net asset value funds with little or no capital to back these operations. Money market funds played a major role in amplifying the crisis after failure of Lehman Brothers that required the US Treasury intervention to offer various forms of support. But as I already noted earlier, reforms in this sector has been incomplete notwithstanding the industry arguments as to why maintaining constant net asset value is so important for corporate America.

The largest constellation of shadow banks are located in the emerging market economies where banks have not been able to reach out to large sections of the population who are eager to finance their way to a better life. In that sense, these shadow banks provide a valuable service to support small business entrepreneurs who cannot easily access bank credit. But shadow banks can also be used as a conduit to make large business loans either to bypass capital requirements when it is made through banks, or because large state owned banks face constraints on lending to certain sectors.

The various types of shadow banking entities include among others: trust companies; microfinance companies; and financial leasing companies. A distinguishing feature of all these entities is the linkages they have with banks and the belief among retail clients that money lent to these entities are as safe as bank deposits, often due to lack of financial literacy. One example is the wealth management products offered by trust companies in China that provide returns linked to a pool of underlying assets. Investors in these products consider them being as safe as bank deposits but yielding a higher return.

At this stage, the total assets of these shadow banking entities in emerging economies is small compared to the banking system assets. Still, these forms of shadow banks pose significant political risks because if there are large scale failures of such entities, it may require a state bailout to rescue the savings of retail clients. Bringing all these non-bank forms of credit intermediation activities under one organisational form so that broad regulatory guidelines for their operations can be drafted and oversight arrangements put in place would be the way forward to build a more resilient financial system in emerging economies.

Let me now turn to the provision of market liquidity by banks against the backdrop of regulatory reforms. Turnover in bond markets are sometimes used as a proxy for market liquidity, and this has reduced substantially in recent years. For example, daily turnover in US Treasury securities amounted to about 12 percent of outstanding debt in 2006. In 2016 the daily turnover was only 3.8 percent of outstanding debt. Some of the reduction in turnover may be linked to the $2.4 trillion worth of Treasury securities held by the Federal Reserve under the quantitative easing program. Reduced turnover in the cash market can also be a consequence of lower trading volumes in repo markets. Daily turnover in the US corporate bond markets, on the other hand, has not changed much. It amounted to about 0.34 percent as a share of outstanding corporate debt in 2006, and in 2016 it was 0.35 percent.

Because a lack of market liquidity can exacerbate asset price falls and these can potentially trigger second round effects that then pose some threats to the resilience of financial markets, regulatory reforms have been blamed for opening up these channels for risk propagation. Even academics have joined this debate and raised important questions as to whether the trade-offs between safeguarding financial stability and tightening regulatory rules are well-balanced. I will provide my views on this debate because there is a trade-off involved, and I will argue that regulatory rules have not got it wrong.

Let me begin with putting the turnover figures in a different perspective. In dollar terms, the annual turnover of marketable US Treasury securities in 2016 amounted to $128.5 trillion. The corresponding figure for US corporate bonds is $7.5 trillion. Typical bid-ask spreads of investment grade corporate bonds for trade sizes between $1 and $5 million is about 4 basis points (0.04 percent). Taking the average maturity of corporate bonds outstanding as 4 years, calculations show that the bid-ask spread for $100 worth of corporate bonds will be 0.16 cents. Bid-ask spreads for US Treasury securities are much lower and is roughly 0.015 cents for $100 worth of Treasuries. Based on these figures, the annual gross fees through bid-ask spreads that banks and broker-dealers can earn if they make markets in US Treasury securities is $19 billion and in the US corporate bonds $12 billion. Lower turnover or trading volumes imply lower revenues for banks. On the flip side, investors stand to gain if they trade less frequently resulting from lower transactions costs involved in portfolio replication.

Does lower trading volumes in US Treasuries and perhaps also in other high grade government bonds imply higher market liquidity risk? The simple answer is that one cannot draw this conclusion based on this information. First, market participants may themselves be trading less, speculating less or adopting a more passive management style to reduce trading costs. Indeed, benefits of active management in US Treasuries are limited and many asset managers tend to offer passive index replication portfolios for government bond markets. Over the last 10 years since the financial crisis erupted, there has been a shift towards passive portfolio replication strategies for well-developed markets. The well-publicised bet by Warren Buffett that a handful of hedge funds will not be able to beat an index fund replicating S&P500 over a 10-year period drives home the point tellingly.

Banks themselves have been allocating less capital to market-making activities and cutting down inventories of their riskier and less liquid assets. This has raised some concerns. Yet the high levels of dealer inventories observed during the run up to the crisis may simply be related to proprietary trading positions rather than to facilitate market-making activities. For example, US primary dealer inventory (net positions) in corporate securities with maturity greater than one year amounted to $40 billion in January 2002, but it rose to $230 billion in December 2007, and it declined to around $55 billion in the second half of 2013. Yet, over this entire period the average daily trading volume for corporate bonds has been in the range $15 to $25 billion.

In light of this observation it is important to ask what the benchmark should be for judging whether trading volumes are now lower. The period 2004 to 2006 is a bad benchmark as risk taking and speculative bets were excessive by any standards. The average daily turnover in US Treasuries between 1996 and 2000 was 6.3 percent, which is higher than 3.8 percent registered in 2016. Beyond the Federal Reserve purchases of Treasuries, the market structure of trading these securities has itself changed, which is likely to depress the reported turnover statistics. Many large investment managers, such as Black Rock and State Street Global Advisors, now employ "crossings" that involve using their internal liquidity to buy and sell securities across different accounts. By developing relationships with other crossing networks, these large asset managers also use external crossings to take advantage of liquidity in the market place. Such portfolio crossings do not enter the turnover statistics I presented above, which is based on trades reported by primary dealers to the Federal Reserve Bank of New York.

To sum up, US primary dealer trading volumes for US Treasuries have fallen, and consequently, dealer inventories are lower. But this does not lead to the conclusion that market liquidity risks, which play an important role in assessing financial market resilience, have risen. If market liquidity dries up, volatility in financial markets will rise. Market volatility remains subdued in recent years implying that liquidity risks have not risen as dealer inventories have fallen. Observed lower dealer inventories can also be a result of binding leverage ratio constraint, which should generally be the case for banks with large investment banking operations. If so, this would confirm that strengthened regulatory rules with complementary minimum capital and leverage ratio requirements are working in tandem to rein in risks from different banking business models. That is what it was designed to do.

Let me now turn to the euro area banking sector where challenges to restoring bank lending capacity in many Member States remain significant. Banks in the euro area finance more than 75 percent of all private sector credit demand. This is in sharp contrast to the United States where banks supply less than 25 percent of private sector credit demand. The reliance on the supply of bank intermediated credit in the euro area means that health of bank balance sheets is an essential precondition for reviving growth.

What are the general criteria used to assess soundness of bank balance sheets? Beyond bank capital ratios, balance sheet strength is usually measured by the ratio of non-performing loans (NPLs) to gross outstanding loans and the capacity of banks to transform excess liquidity they hold into loans to the private sector. The lower the NPL ratio and higher the capacity to supply loans, stronger is the banks' balance sheet. Usually a high NPL ratio constrains banks' capacity to lend as they continue to consume bank capital until they are disposed. In turn this affects bank profitability, which is an additional indicator of bank balance sheet strength.

Let me begin with some statistics on NPLs in selected euro area countries. In Greece and Cyprus, the NPL ratios in the second half of 2016 were close to 50 percent. At these levels of NPL ratios, banks are effectively not capable of meeting the credit needs of the economy. In Portugal and Slovenia NPL ratios are close to 20 percent, whereas in Ireland and Italy they are around 17 percent. For Spanish banks the NPL ratio is 6 percent, but if a category called performing forborne loans (FBLs) are included, the combined ratio of NPLs and FBLs exceed 9.5 percent. Spain is an exception in the euro area with such a high FBL ratio, and it raises some questions as to whether they stem from forbearance measures applied by banks to avoid the debtor becoming non-performing. In layman terms, it means a bank might extend a loan to enable a debtor to pay interest due on outstanding loans. To put the NPL ratios in perspective, in the second half of 2016 the aggregate NPL ratio of US banks was less than 2 percent. Healthy banking systems have NPL ratios (as a share of gross outstanding loans) between 1 and 3 percent.

The NPLs can be drilled down further to assess what types of debtor claims show high default rates. This can provide insights into what types of public policy responses might be most effective to reviving growth in these economies by restoring banks' capacity to lend. When bank loans are segregated into three categories – loans to small and medium-sized enterprises (SMEs), loans to large corporates, and loans to households – NPL ratios for SMEs are uniformly high in all the above euro area countries. For example, in Ireland, Italy and Portugal about 30 percent of all loans given to SMEs are non-performing. In Spain the figure is about 18 percent; Greece and Cyprus have nearly 65 percent of their SME loans in non-performing category.

Why have banks not managed to off-load their large share of non-performing SME loans? The general problems facing euro area banks to get rid of their NPLs are the lengthy and expensive judiciary processes compounded by the lack of markets for NPLs and their associated collaterals. Focusing more narrowly on SMEs, bank loans to this sector are usually backed by collateral with real estate being the most common. Unlike in the United States, foreclosures of mortgage collateral can be lengthy and subject to legal hurdles given weak debt enforcement frameworks and a lack of deep and liquid markets for distressed assets. Moreover, following a long period of low growth and low inflation, valuations used by banks for mortgage collateral based on market prices may not reflect liquidation values. But some progress has been made in this area with many countries taking initiatives to reform their legal systems to accelerate foreclosures and promote institutional arrangements for out of court settlement.

A further problem confronting euro area banks to off-load non-performing SME loans is that many SMEs are family run businesses. Finding alternative buyers to takeover and run the SMEs after restructuring them will also face challenges. As a consequence the residual franchise value of the business may be limited with obvious implications for recovery value on outstanding loans. This in turn will encourage forbearance and discourage asset disposals.

In addition, there are also other reasons that may deter banks' willingness to shed NPLs. Accounting standards, for example, can dampen banks' willingness to reduce their non-performing loans when recovery values are expected to be lower than their carrying values in the loan book. Provisioning requirements under current financial accounting standards use a backward-looking incurred loss approach that can lead to delayed loan loss recognition. In addition, the IFRS accounting standards followed in the EU allow banks to book the accrual of interest income on NPLs even if the bank is not receiving some or all of the cash income due on the loans. These accounting practices have effectively provided disincentives for banks in the euro area countries reporting under IFRS to reduce their stock of NPLs. Starting in January 2018, new standards (IFRS 9) will apply that require forward-looking provisioning based on expected losses which could alter incentives. Still, even under the new standards, banks can continue to record interest income on NPLs. Banks in the United States, which are required to follow the US GAAP accounting standards, are not allowed to accrue interest on NPLs. This encourages them to shed NPLs more quickly than their European counterparts.

Let me now turn to another question. Why is a large stock of non-performing SME loans more problematic than other loans? This is because SMEs have an important bearing on the level of real economic activity in the euro area. SMEs constitute about 98 percent of all euro area firms and employ about 70 percent of the workforce. Most SMEs are funded through bank loans or bank-intermediated trade credit. This reliance makes SMEs vulnerable to deterioration in bank balance sheets. At the same time, banks themselves come under stress when the health of SMEs is poor following an extended period of depressed macroeconomic growth. Restoring banks' capacity to lend by helping them to off-load their NPLs essentially translates to reviving SMEs' ability to contribute to growth and employment while monetary policy remains accommodative during the adjustment period.

Postponing reforms to address problems facing the banking sector in countries with high NPL ratios risks dragging these countries into an extended period of low growth, low inflation, and high unemployment. The adoption of IFRS 9 standards in 2018 will further depress banks' capital ratios due to increased loss provisioning requirements. Until banks reduce their stock of NPLs, bank profitability will remain low delaying recapitalisation of banks through retained profits. Raising equity from investors in this environment is going to be difficult. Quantitative easing, long-term refinancing operations and negative deposits rates on excess bank reserves to encourage lending introduced by ECB are medicines that help buy time and reduce pain, but they cannot cure the banking sector problems in many euro area countries that are essential to restoring growth and employment. Indeed, monetary policy transmission channels are through bank balance sheets, and more so in the euro area reliant on bank-intermediated credit. For effectiveness of this transmission mechanism, healthy bank balance sheets are a pre-requisite. That is not the case now.

This leads us to my next question. Can public policy initiatives address the problems facing several euro area banking systems stemming from a large stock of non-performing loans? The answer is yes as institutional frameworks are available even if some tweaks to existing legal frameworks are needed for the initiative. To some extent, the success of such an initiative will also depend on the conservativeness of banks' provisioning practices for NPLs. Let me provide some thoughts on how public policy can address the challenges facing the banking sector in several euro area countries even if reaching political consensus might be difficult.

A first step towards this goal would be to setup an asset management company (AMC) that is centrally coordinated at the euro area level. Banks in countries with high share of NPLs should be obliged to transfer them to the AMC until they reach a target NPL ratio level of 4 or 5 percent. The most difficult part of the exercise will be agreeing on what the transfer price for the assets will be when sold to the AMC (that is, the price at which NPLs will be bought by the AMC). As I mentioned earlier, if banks had been under-provisioning by using inflated recovery values for the non-performing assets, it will force banks to realise the actual losses when the asset transfers are made. This clearly will discourage banks to voluntarily participate in the balance sheet clean-up program. Still, bank resolution tools can be employed to recapitalise banks when there is a capital shortfall resulting from the asset transfers made based on expected liquidation values. It will be a test to see if euro area governments can put words into deeds. For a start, banks that are coming under the single supervisory mechanism can be targeted given a more unified framework employed for valuation and provisioning practices of these banks.

Based on the levels of NPLs held by banks, the book value of NPLs to be transferred could amount to about €500 billion. Coverage ratio on these loans average around 45 percent, and this implies that these assets could be transferred at 55 percent of the book value amounting to €275 billion. This in turn is the amount of funding that the AMC will need to buy the non-performing assets. One option for raising these funds would be for the European Stability Mechanism (ESM) to issue notes backed by the assets of the AMC, which would then be passed on to banks in exchange for the NPLs transferred. But this would require a treaty change as existing rules only allow funding to be provided to an ESM Member State under the form of stability support to recapitalise a financial institution. Alternatively, the AMC could issue bonds in the capital markets, but this will be more expensive and banks would not get sufficient capital relief when repaid through these bonds unless these bonds have appropriate sovereign or supranational guarantees to lower their risk weights.

Additional equity capital for the AMC needed to bear losses under a range of macroeconomic scenarios would have to be paid by Member States. To reduce moral hazard, Member States could be asked to contribute to the equity capital as a proportion of the NPLs transferred to the AMC by banks in their jurisdiction. Encouraging participation of private investors will reduce the contributions Member States will have to make towards equity capital. By centralising the resources in one institution for the resolution and restructuring of troubled loans, significant operational efficiency can be achieved. At the same time, banks will regain balance sheet capacity to extend new credit to viable firms and support economic recovery. This will also help the private sector to repair their balance sheets and entrepreneurs to pursue new business projects. In terms of the size of public sector funds needed for capitalising the AMC, this will be much lower than what was required for the Capital Purchase Program under which the US Treasury provided capital amounting to $220 billion to more than 700 viable financial institutions in exchange for preferred stocks or warrants.

Let me now turn to the medium term risks I see to the financial system. Almost every other day, we read news items about pension schemes and the difficult adjustments that are needed to make them sustainable over the medium and long term. The difficult adjustments refer to the cuts in our retirement income stream needed to ensure that they can be paid. Introducing such cuts to pension rights that have already been acquired is not legally enforceable in many countries including in most US States. This remains the major bottleneck to reforming pension schemes as the burden of making them sustainable will fall on the younger generation. That is politically unpalatable and constrains any meaningful reforms to be undertaken.

How are pension schemes organised? In many countries, pension provision is covered by a mandatory public scheme (usually referred to as social security schemes), which is often supplemented by occupational private pension schemes. The extent to which occupational pension schemes supplement public schemes varies substantially among advanced economies. Among public pension schemes, some are funded, that is the pension liabilities are backed by pension assets; others are unfunded and referred to as pay-as-you-go (PAYG) schemes, that is the current pension payments are financed from contributions or payroll taxes paid by current employees.

Occupational pension schemes can be broadly classified into defined benefit (DB) schemes and defined contribution (DC) schemes. DB schemes offer the employees more measurable post-employment income benefits; but they lack the portability that DC schemes offer employees when they switch employers. In a DC plan, the amount of money that has to be contributed to the fund is specified, but the benefits payout will be known only at the time of retirement.

What exactly are the risks facing pension funds? As we all know, lower macroeconomic growth translates to lower returns on financial assets. This means that returns on pension fund assets are going to be lower going forward. Improvements in health care have increased our longevity by more than year compared to a few decades back, and this is likely to rise further. As this implies that we will receive pension payments for a longer period of time than our uncles and parents, the liabilities of pension funds have risen. For pension assets to keep up with pension liabilities, our contributions to the pension fund will have to increase to avoid build-up of deficits. This is the case for DB schemes where the employee has a contractual right to receive a certain percent of last drawn salary or an average of the last years of salary as retirement income stream. These pension liabilities are included in the balance sheet of the employer and are non-negotiable (under current law). The only way the employer can default on the payments is by filing for bankruptcy. That is not an option available to a local government.

These challenges also confront public pension schemes that are designed as PAYG schemes. The return on the notional assets (because they are unfunded) is equal to the growth rate of the GDP. When macroeconomic growth is subdued, they face the same problems as any other DB scheme as adjustments to already accrued pension benefits is not enforceable. But public pension schemes face even greater difficulties because in an extended period of low macroeconomic growth, unemployment levels are also higher. That translates to lower contributions from pay-roll, and the deficits will have to be funded by issuing government debt.

Risks to the sustainability of existing pension arrangements, particularly when they are of the defined benefit scheme type, are being highlighted in the press regularly. To provide a sense of the magnitude of these risks, let me give some illustrative numbers. Let us suppose a DB pension scheme carries out the valuation of the liabilities under the assumption that the return on pension assets will be 7 percent per annum, and under this assumption pension assets equal pension liabilities. What happens if the lower growth scenario requires adjusting the expected return on assets down to 6 percent per annum? With a typical average duration (similar to maturity) of pension liabilities of 15 years, the one percentage point lower returns will translate to a 15 percent pension deficit.

Faced with this dilemma, many state pension schemes that are backed by assets tend to overstate the returns that can be generated. In practice, the employer will have to make up for the deficit of 15 percent of total liabilities and impose higher pension contributions to be made by their employees in order to receive the promised pension benefits. By how much should the contributions increase if the expected return on assets is one percentage point lower? This requires the use of an actuarial model, and the estimate turns out to be roughly about 5 to 6 percentage points. That is, if the combined employee plus employer contributions have been 20 percent of the pensionable salary, the new combined contributions will have to be at least 25 percent of the pensionable salary. Clearly, there will be no incentive from the employee side that the employer uses a more conservative assumption for expected asset returns of the pension fund if the increase in contributions has to be equally shared.

The disincentive among all parties to address the problems associated with the build-up of pension deficits is simply delaying essential reforms needed to put many pension schemes on a sustainable footing over the long term. For a number of public pension schemes offering defined benefits, the wakeup call that they are not sustainable will occur when markets do not buy the debt issued by the local state or the sovereign government that is required to fund the widening deficits on pension commitments. This may ultimately force new laws to be introduced to make the unpalatable adjustments needed to reduce the burden on the next generation of employees. But if Greece is a representative example, we should expect more trouble on the streets in Europe over the medium term.

www.ingramcontent.com/pod-product-compliance
Lightning Source LLC
Chambersburg PA
CBHW030509210326
41597CB00013B/847